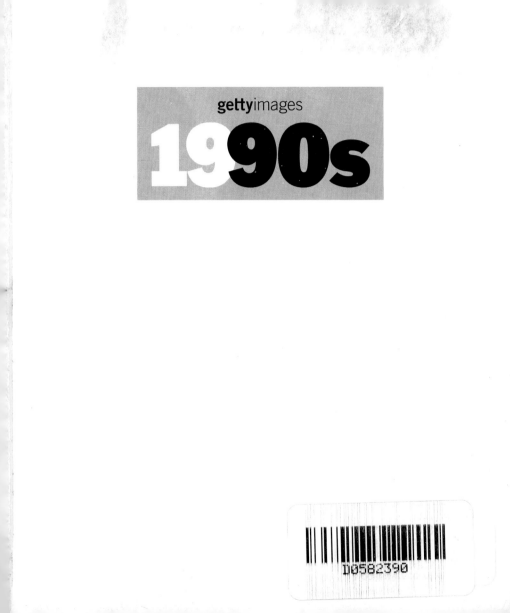

gettyimages

1990s

D0582390

Decades of the 20th Century
Dekaden des 20. Jahrhunderts
Décennies du XXe siècle

Nick Yapp

KÖNEMANN

This edition ©KÖNEMANN*, an imprint of Tandem Verlag GmbH, Königswinter
Photographs ©2001 Getty Images

This book was produced by Getty Images
Unique House, 21–31 Woodfield Road, London W9 2BA

For KÖNEMANN*:
Managing editor: Sally Bald
Project editors: Lucile Bas, Meike Hilbring
Translation into German: Oliver Fröschke
Translation into French: Arnaud Dupin de Beyssat

For Getty Images:
Art director: Michael Rand
Design: Tea McAleer
Picture editor: Ali Khoja
Editor: Richard Collins
Proof reader: Liz Ihre

*KÖNEMANN is a registered trademark of Tandem Verlag GmbH

Printed in Germany

ISBN 3-8331-1085-6

10 9 8 7 6 5 4 3 2 1
X IX VIII VII VI V IV III II I

Frontispiece: A column of refugees from Kosovo trudge up Likej Mountain on
their way to Macedonia, 30 March 1999. Their route was later blocked by the
Macedonian army until UNHCR officials exerted pressure on the Macedonian
government.

Frontispiz: Flüchtlinge aus dem Kosovo besteigen auf ihrem Weg nach Mazedonien
den Berg Likej, 30. März 1999. Sie wurden später von der mazedonischen Armee so
lange aufgehalten, bis offizielle Mitglieder der UNHCR Druck auf die mazedonische
Regierung ausübten.

Frontispice : Des réfugiés du Kosovo escaladent la montagne Likej pour se rendre
en Macédonie, le 30 mars 1999. Leur route a été bloquée plus tard par l'armée
macédonienne jusqu'à ce que les officiels de l'UNHCR fassent pression sur le
gouvernement macédonien.

Contents / Inhalt / Sommaire

Introduction

The Iron Curtain that had separated East from West for forty years was wrenched open. The Berlin Wall was smashed. Mechanical worms ground their way beneath the Channel, directly linking France and Britain for the first time in history. The Market Economy marched from strength to strength, though banks collapsed and stock exchanges hiccoughed alarmingly. In the United States, many people burnt their fingers on the latest hot properties – junk bonds. Much of Europe bound its fortunes to the new euro, while others stood by… watching, waiting and biting their nails.

Germany was reunited. In South Africa, black and white laid aside the worst of their prejudices under the wise guidance of Nelson Mandela. The old Soviet Empire fell apart. Yugoslavia tore itself to pieces. North and South Korea edged cautiously together. It was as though the tectonic plates of the earth's crust were moving uneasily as the end of the second Christian Millennium approached.

War in the Gulf brought lasting fame to 'Stormin'' Norman Schwarzkopf and Colin Powell, and momentary 'newsworthiness' to the Kurds. War in Chechnya brought misery to thousands and fame to no one. The *annus horribilis* of 1992 provoked that rare phenomenon – a royal grumble – though there were no problems in Queen Elizabeth's life that a little family therapy and a good insurance policy could not have solved. President Clinton had eight *anni mirabiles* as US President, and the smiles on his face suggested that he enjoyed every one of them.

Aung San Suu Kyi condemned the military dictatorship in Burma; in Pakistan, Benazir Bhutto was dismissed by the military. Voters in Britain supported John Major in 1992, but later rejected him in favour of New Labour's Tony Blair. Iitzhak Rabin, Prime Minister of Israel, was assassinated by a Jewish law student. Seven years after his mother's assassination, Rajiv Gandhi of India was killed by a woman who had strapped explosives to her own body.

Having announced in 1987 that he was 'bad', Michael Jackson gave people the chance to agree with him. The cult of celebrity reached new and awesome heights with the creation of 'boy' and 'girl' bands, who shot to instant fame on the basis of a single well-plugged album. Hollywood regained much of its old glamour. The number of television channels available multiplied like germs on a rotting corpse. To the masses, sport became as important as real life, as did the adventures of soap stars to millions more.

There were new inventions, new diseases, natural disasters, bombings, hijackings, deeds of high bravery and examples of crass stupidity. But the stubborn, silly, punch-drunk and wonderful human race somehow blundered on to the end of the decade, the end of the century and the end of the Millennium.

Einführung

Der Eiserne Vorhang, der Ost und West über 40 Jahre lang getrennt hatte, wurde aufgerissen. Die Berliner Mauer fiel. Mechanische Maulwürfe gruben sich ihren Weg unter dem Ärmelkanal, um Frankreich und Großbritannien zum ersten Mal in der Geschichte direkt miteinander zu verbinden. Und obwohl Bankhäuser in Konkurs gingen und Finanzmärkte mitunter gefährlich röchelten, marschierte die Marktwirtschaft unaufhaltsam von einem Hoch zum nächsten. In den USA verbrannten sich viele Anleger an den neuen „junk bonds" – Billig-Anleihen – die Finger. Große Teile Europas legten ihr Schicksal in die Hände des neuen Euro, während andere untätig blieben, der Entwicklung zusahen und an den Nägeln kauten …

Deutschland wurde wiedervereinigt. Unter der weisen Führung Nelson Mandelas gaben die weißen und schwarzen Südafrikaner die schlimmsten ihrer Vorurteile auf. Das alte Sowjetische Reich fiel auseinander. Jugoslawien zerstückelte sich selbst in seine Einzelteile. Nord- und Südkorea näherten sich vorsichtig einander an. Die tektonischen Erdplatten schienen sich gegen Ende des zweiten Jahrtausends christlicher Zeitrechnung unruhig zu bewegen.

Durch den Golfkrieg kamen der „Wüstenstürmer" Norman Schwarzkopf und Colin Powell zu anhaltendem Ruhm, während die Kurdenfrage nur vorübergehenden Nachrichtenwert besaß. Der Krieg in Tschetschenien brachte Elend über Tausende und Ruhm für Niemanden. 1992 – das *annus horribilis* – brachte das seltene Phänomen des „königlichen Grolls" (Royal Grumble) hervor, und das, obwohl es im Leben der Queen Elizabeth II. keine Probleme gab, die mit einer kleinen Familientherapie oder einer guten Versicherungspolice nicht zu lösen gewesen wären. Clinton dagegen hatte als US-Präsident acht *anni mirabiles* und das Lächeln auf seinem Gesicht lässt ahnen, dass er jedes einzelne davon genossen hat.

Aung San Suu Kyi verurteilte die Militärdiktatur in Burma; in Pakistan wurde Benazir Bhutto durch das Militär abgesetzt. Die britischen Wähler stimmten 1992 für John Major, nur um ihn später zu Gunsten Tony Blairs und seiner New-Labour-Partei wieder abzuwählen. Israels Premierminister Itzhak Rabin wurde von einem jüdischen Jurastudenten ermordet. Sieben Jahre nach der Ermordung seiner Mutter fiel Rajiv Gandhi dem Selbstmordattentat einer Frau zum Opfer, die sich Sprengstoff auf den Körper geschnallt hatte.

Michael Jacksons Bekenntnis schlecht zu sein („I'm Bad") aus dem Jahre 1987 gab den Leuten die Gelegenheit zur Zustimmung. Der Starkult erreichte einen neuen und Schwindel erregenden Höhepunkt, als die so genannten „Boy- und Girlgroups" auf der Basis eines geschickt promoteten Albums zu plötzlichem Ruhm aufstiegen. Hollywood gewann einiges von seinem alten Glamour zurück. Die Zahl der Fernsehkanäle vermehrte sich wie Keime in einem verwesenden Leichnam. Sport wurde für das Massenpublikum so wichtig wie das wahre Leben und die Abenteuer der Seifenoper-Stars zogen Millionen in ihren Bann.

Es gab neue Erfindungen, neue Krankheiten, Naturkatastrophen, Bombenanschläge, Flugzeugentführungen, Taten von großem Mut und Beispiele krasser Dummheit. Zwischen all dem taumelte die menschliche Rasse – hartnäckig, unbelehrbar und wundervoll wie sie ist – auf das Ende der Dekade zu. Und damit dem Ende des Jahrhunderts und des Jahrtausends entgegen.

Introduction

Le rideau de fer qui isolait l'Est de l'Ouest depuis quarante ans avait été soulevé de force et le mur de Berlin détruit. Des taupes mécaniques creusaient sous la Manche, reliant directement la France et la Grande-Bretagne pour la première fois de leur histoire. L'économie de marché se renforçait malgré les faillites des banques et les soubresauts alarmants des bourses. Aux États-Unis, beaucoup se brûlaient les doigts avec les junk bonds, les nouvelles valeurs mobilières. Une partie de l'Europe liait sa fortune au nouvel euro tandis que l'autre patientait… observant, attendant et se rongeant les ongles.

L'Allemagne était réunifiée. En Afrique du Sud, les Blancs et les Noirs abandonnaient leurs pires antagonismes sous la sage autorité de Nelson Mandela. Le vieil Empire soviétique s'écroulait. La Yougoslavie éclatait en mille morceaux. Les Corée du Nord et du Sud se rapprochaient avec circonspection l'une de l'autre. Le monde bougeait comme si les plaques politiques de la croûte terrestre s'agitaient à la fin du second millénaire chrétien.

La guerre du Golfe apportait une notoriété durable à « Stormin' » Norman Schwarzkopf et Colin Powell, et faisait momentanément de la « publicité » aux Kurdes. La guerre en Tchétchénie engendrait la souffrance de milliers de personnes sans apporter la célébrité à quiconque. L'*annus horribilis* de 1992 provoquait un phénomène rare : les lamentations de la famille royale britannique – bien qu'il n'y eût aucun problème dans la vie de la reine Elizabeth qu'une petite thérapie familiale et une bonne police d'assurance n'auraient pu résoudre. Clinton avait connu huit *anni mirabiles* au titre de président des États-Unis, les sourires qu'il arborait témoignant qu'il avait bien profité de chacune d'entre elles.

Aung San Suu Kyi condamnait la dictature militaire en Birmanie, et, au Pakistan, Benazir Bhutto était renversée par les militaires. Les électeurs britanniques qui avaient soutenu John Major en 1992 le rejetèrent ensuite en faveur de Tony Blair, du nouveau Parti travailliste. Iitzhak Rabin, Premier ministre d'Israël, était assassiné par un étudiant en droit juif. En Inde, sept ans après le meurtre de sa mère, Rajiv Gandhi était tué par une femme qui s'était entouré le corps d'explosifs.

Après avoir annoncé en 1987 qu'il était « mauvais », Michael Jackson donnait à son public l'occasion de le constater. La soif de popularité atteignait de nouvelles et surprenantes hauteurs avec la création de boys et de girls band qui connaissaient une gloire instantanée grâce à un seul album bien distribué et matraqué. Hollywood retrouvait une bonne part de son prestige passé. Le nombre de chaînes de télévision se multipliait comme des mouches sur un cadavre. Pour les masses, le sport – ou les aventures des stars de feuilletons – devenait aussi essentiel que la vie réelle.

Il y avait de nouvelles inventions, de nouvelles maladies, des désastres naturels, des bombardements, des enlèvements, des exploits et des manifestations de franche ineptie. Mais la race humaine, tout obstinée, stupide, abrutie et merveilleuse qu'elle soit, parvenait tant bien que mal à atteindre la fin de la décennie, la fin du siècle et la fin du millénaire.

1. Movers and shakers
Spieler und Gegenspieler
Progressistes et agitateurs

A shaky start. President Bill Clinton grimaces as his translation
device fails at the beginning of his joint press conference with the
Russian President Boris Yeltsin, Helsinki, 21 March 1997.

Ein wackeliger Start. Präsident Bill Clinton kommentiert den
Ausfall seiner Übersetzungshilfe zu Beginn einer gemeinsamen
Pressekonferenz mit dem russischen Präsidenten Boris Jelzin mit
einer Grimasse, Helsinki, 21. März 1997.

Des débuts incertains. La subite panne de son casque de traduction
simultanée a rendu perplexe le président Bill Clinton lors de la
conférence de presse qu'il tenait avec le président russe Boris Eltsine
à Helsinki, le 21 mars 1997.

1. Movers and shakers
Spieler und Gegenspieler
Progressistes et agitateurs

It was a decade of change and replacement, of separation and new alliances. Nelson and Winnie Mandela, the Prince and Princess of Wales, Mikhail Gorbachev and the Russian people – all agreed to part. Mandela and Buthelezi attempted to find common ground to unite their peoples in South Africa. Iitzhak Rabin and Yasser Arafat came to an accord at Camp David. A new government in Britain brought Nationalists and Unionists to within spitting distance of each other in Northern Ireland.

Kohl and Mitterrand were replaced by Schröder and Chirac. Clinton replaced Bush. Yeltsin replaced Gorbachev. Also among the replacement heroes were the newly-elected President Walesa of Poland and President Havel of Czechoslovakia.

The Cold War came to an end, but there were plenty of new villains on the block. Saddam Hussein was considered the most scurrilous but proved elusive. General Manuel Noriega of Panama was more easily apprehended and packed off to gaol. Slobodan Milosevic of Serbia and Colonel Gaddafi of Libya proved far more intractable. The new villains rivalled their forerunners for obstinacy, as far as the West was concerned.

Die neunziger Jahre waren eine Dekade des Wandels und der Ablösung, der Trennung und neuer Allianzen. Nelson und Winnie Mandela, Prinz Charles und Prinzessin Diana, Michail Gorbatschow und das russische Volk – alle willigten ein, getrennte Wege zu gehen. Mandela und Buthelezi unternahmen den Versuch, eine gemeinsame Basis für die Vereinigung ihrer Völker in Südafrika zu finden. Itzhak Rabin und Yassir Arafat kamen in Camp David zu einer historischen Einigung. Eine neue britische Regierung vermochte es, die Kluft zwischen nordirischen Nationalisten und Unionisten auf ein Minimum zu verringern.

Kohl und Mitterand wurden von Schröder und Chirac abgelöst. Clinton ersetzte Bush. Jelzin kam für Gorbatschow. Zu Helden der politischen Wachablösung wurden darüber hinaus die neu gewählten Präsidenten von Polen und Tschechien, Walesa und Havel.

Der Kalte Krieg wurde zwar beendet, doch neue Störenfriede betraten die Szene: Saddam Hussein galt als der garstigste von allen; aber wie sich herausstellte, war er schwer zu fassen. Panamas General Manuel Noriega war leichter zu verhaften und einzusperren. Um einiges widerspenstiger zeigten sich dagegen Serbiens Slobodan Milosevic und der libysche Revolutionsführer Gaddafi. Was den Westen betrifft, standen diese „neuen Störenfriede" ihren Vorgängern in puncto Eigensinn in nichts nach.

C'était la décennie des changements et des remplacements, des séparations et des nouvelles alliances. Nelson et Winnie Mandela, le prince et la princesse de Galles, Mikhail Gorbatchev et le peuple russe étaient tous d'accord pour rompre. En Afrique du Sud, Mandela et Buthelezi tentaient de trouver un terrain commun pour unifier leurs peuples. Iitzhak Rabin et Yasser Arafat parvenaient à s'entendre à Camp David. En Grande-Bretagne, un nouveau gouvernement rapprochait Nationalistes et Unionistes d'Irlande du Nord.

Kohl et Mitterand étaient remplacés par Schröder et Chirac. Clinton succédait à Bush. Eltsine remplaçait Gorbatchev. Les héros Walesa, nouveau président élu de Pologne, et Havel, président de Tchécoslovaquie, prenaient également la relève.

Si la guerre froide touchait à sa fin, il restait encore beaucoup de nouveaux méchants. Saddam Hussein, considéré comme le plus virulent, se révéla insaisissable. Le général Manuel Noriega, de Panama, se fit plus facilement appréhender et jeter en prison. Slobodan Milosevic, en Serbie, et le colonel Kadhafi, en Libye, se montrèrent plus intraitables. Ces nouveaux bandits rivalisaient d'obstination avec leurs prédécesseurs jusqu'à ce que l'Occident se sente vraiment concerné.

ULLI MICHEL/REUTERS/ARCHIVE PHOTOS

The end of a bitter age. Nelson and Winnie Mandela greet the crowds waiting outside Victor Verster Prison, Paarl, South Africa, 11 February 1990. It was Mandela's first day of freedom for twenty-seven years.

Das Ende eines bitteren Zeitalters. Nelson und Winnie Mandela begrüßen die vor dem Victor-Verster-Gefängnis wartende Menge, Paarl, Südafrika, 11. Februar 1990. Es war Mandelas erster Tag in Freiheit nach 27-jähriger Gefangenschaft.

La fin d'une période noire. Nelson et Winnie Mandela saluent la foule massée à l'extérieur de la prison Victor Verster de Paarl, en Afrique du Sud, le 11 février 1990. C'était le premier jour de liberté de Mandela depuis 27 ans.

JOAO SILVA/BLACK STAR/COLORIFIC!

KwaZulu Chief Minister Buthelezi (left), with Zulu King Zwelethini, Ngoma, Africa. Buthelezi is also president and co-founder of the paramilitary Inkatha, by turn ally and opponent of Mandela.

Buthelezi (links), Chefminister von KwaZulu und Zulukönig Zwelethini in Ngoma, Afrika. Buthelezi ist gleichzeitig Chef und Mitbegründer der paramilitärischen Inkatha, abwechselnd Gegner und Verbündeter Mandelas.

Le Premier ministre du Kwazulu, Buthelezi (à gauche), et le roi Zoulou Zwelethini se rencontrent à Ngoma (Afrique). Buthelezi était également le président et cofondateur du parti paramilitaire Inkatha, tour à tour allié et adversaire de Mandela.

DAVID BRAUCHLI/LIAISON AGENCY

The hands of democracy. Nelson Mandela reaches out to voters at the Ikageng
Stadium, Potchefstroom, Transvaal, 31 January 1994. He was campaigning in the
first all-race democratic election in South Africa.

Die Hände der Demokratie. Nelson Mandela beschwört die im Ikageng-Stadion
von Potchefstroom, Transvaal, versammelten Wähler im Zuge seines Wahlkampfs
für die ersten freien und demokratischen Wahlen in Südafrika, 31. Januar 1994.

Les mains de la démocratie. Nelson Mandela étend les bras vers les électeurs
réunis au Ikageng Stadium, à Potchefstroom, dans le Transvaal, le 31 janvier 1994.
Il faisait campagne pour la première élection démocratique et multiraciale organisée
en Afrique du Sud.

DAVID BRAUCHLI/LIAISON AGENCY

President F W de Klerk on a campaign rally at Dwarsfontein, Western Transvaal, 21 January 1994. The election was still three months away but the days of white rule were numbered.

Präsident F. W. de Klerk bei einer Wahlkampfveranstaltung in Dwarsfontein, West-Transvaal, 21. Januar 1994. Obwohl die Wahlen erst drei Monate später stattfanden, waren die Tage weißer Herrschaft bereits gezählt.

Le président F. W. de Klerk en tournée électorale à Dwarsfontein, dans le Transvaal occidental, le 21 janvier 1994. L'élection aura lieu dans trois mois mais les jours du pouvoir blanc sont déjà comptés.

EPA/PA

Praying for Allah's help. President Saddam Hussein pauses during a tour of villages in northern Iraq, 29 March 1998. The sympathetic portrait was released by the Iraqi News Agency.

Beten um Allahs Hilfe. Präsident Saddam Hussein in einem Moment der Besinnung während seiner Reise durch den Norden von Irak, 29. März 1998. Das sympathische Porträt wurde von der irakischen Nachrichtenagentur verbreitet.

Prier pour obtenir l'aide d'Allah. Le président Saddam Hussein interrompt sa tournée des villages du nord de l'Irak, le 29 mars 1998. Ce sympathique portrait fut diffusé par la Iraqi News Agency.

WALLY McNAMEE/WOODFIN CAMP & ASSOCIATES/COLORIFIC!

Praying for Allied help. President George Bush visits Allied troops during the Gulf War early in 1991. The fighting lasted only four days, the dying considerably longer.

Beten um alliierte Hilfe. Der Präsident George Bush besucht alliierte Truppen während des Golfkrieges Anfang 1991. Die Kampfhandlungen dauerten nur vier Tage, das Sterben deutlich länger.

Prier pour obtenir l'aide des Alliés. Le président George Bush rend visite aux troupes alliées pendant la guerre du Golfe, début 1991. Les combats ne durèrent que quatre jours, les dommages bien plus longtemps.

Careless rapture! Lech Walesa greets supporters during the Polish presidential election campaign, Cracow, 1990. His jubilation was premature but not misplaced: the former leader of Solidarity was elected.

Sorglose Begeisterung! Lech Walesa grüßt seine Anhänger in Krakau während des Präsidentschaftswahlkampfes 1990. Der Jubel kam zwar verfrüht, aber zu Recht: Der ehemalige Führer der Gewerkschaft Solidarität konnte die Wahl gewinnen.

Une joie insouciante ! Lech Walesa salue ses supporters à Cracovie pendant la campagne des élections présidentielles polonaises, en 1990. Sa jubilation était prématurée mais prémonitoir : l'ancien dirigeant de Solidarnosc fut en effet élu.

Careful consideration. President Vaclav Havel of Czechoslovakia critically monitors his performance on a television set in Lany, 1990. He had become president the previous year, six months after being released from prison.

Sorgfältige Prüfung. Kritisch beäugt der tschechoslowakische Präsident Vaclav Havel einen seiner Fernsehauftritte, Lany, 1990. Ein Jahr zuvor war er zum Präsidenten gewählt worden, nur sechs Monate nach seiner Haftentlassung.

Une attention soucieuse. Vaclav Havel, président de la Tchécoslovaquie, regarde d'un œil critique sa prestation télévisée, à Lany en 1990. Il avait été élu l'année précédente, six mois après sa sortie de prison.

EPA/PA

Maintaining the old order. China's most powerful man, Deng Xiaoping, watches a fireworks display, 1 October 1994. He was 90 years old and head of the most populous country in the world.

Die alte Ordnung aufrechterhalten. Chinas mächtigster Mann, Deng Xiaoping, beobachtet ein Feuerwerk, 1. Oktober 1994. Deng war zu diesem Zeitpunkt 90 Jahre alt und stand immer noch an der Spitze des bevölkerungsreichsten Lands der Erde.

Maintenir l'ordre ancien. Le « chef suprême » de la Chine, Deng Xiaoping, assiste à un feu d'artifice le 1ᵉʳ octobre 1994. Il avait 90 ans et dirigeait le pays le plus peuplé du monde.

EPA/PA

Keeper of the revolution. Fidel Castro faces the media at the 9th Ibero-American Summit, Havana, Cuba, 16 November 1999. For more than forty years he has guided his country's fortunes.

Hüter der Revolution. Fidel Castro stellt sich den Medien beim neunten Ibero-Amerikanischen Gipfeltreffen in Havanna, Kuba, 16. November 1999. Seit über 40 Jahren lenkt Castro die Geschicke seines Landes.

Gardien de la Révolution. Fidel Castro face aux médias lors du 9ᵉ Sommet ibéro-américain à la Havane (Cuba), le 16 novembre 1999. Il a tenu les rênes de son pays pendant plus de 40 ans.

Time magazine's portrait of Slobodan Milosevic, 8 June 1992. He had just been re-elected President of Serbia, amid accusations of fraud.

Ein Porträt Slobodan Milosevics aus dem Magazin *Time* vom 8. Juni 1992. Soeben wurde er, trotz Betrugsvorwürfen, als Präsident Serbiens wieder gewählt.

Le portrait de Slobodan Milosevic, paru dans le magazine *Time* du 8 juin 1992. Il venait d'être réélu président de Serbie malgré des accusations de fraude électorale.

HRVOJE POLAN/LIAISON AGENCY

Franjo Tudjman, President of Croatia, on the stump during a pre-election rally of his Croatian Democratic Party (HDZ) in Zagreb's main square, 22 June 1997. The Yugoslavian Republic had irreparably broken apart.

Der kroatische Präsident Franjo Tudjman während einer Rede beim Wahlkampf für seine Partei HDZ (Demokratische Partei Kroatiens) auf dem Zentralplatz von Zagreb, 22. Juni 1997. Die Republik Jugoslawien war bereits unwiederbringlich auseinander gebrochen.

Franjo Tudjman, président de Croatie, fait campagne sur la grande place de Zagreb, le 22 juin 1997, lors d'une tournée préélectorale pour le Parti démocrate de Croatie (HDZ). La fracture de la République yougoslave était irrémédiablement consommée.

RICK FRIEDMAN/BLACK STAR/COLORIFIC!

Happy days… Bill and Hillary Clinton share a moment of joy in
New Hampshire during the 1992 campaign to elect a Democratic
candidate for the presidency.

Glückliche Tage … Bill und Hillary Clinton amüsieren sich gemeinsam
bei einer Veranstaltung in New Hampshire im Rahmen der Kandidaten-
kür der Demokratischen Partei vor den Präsidentschaftswahlen 1992.

Des jours heureux … Bill et Hillary Clinton dans un moment d'hilarité
lors de la campagne de 1992 dans le New Hampshire pour l'élection
d'un candidat démocrate à la présidence.

RICHARD ELLIS/LIAISON AGENCY

…but, oh, those lonely nights. Amid rumours of marital separation, the Clintons appear (back to back) at a Millennium evening lecture on 'Women as Citizens' in the East Room of the White House, 15 March 1999.

… einsame Nächte. Die Clintons (Rücken an Rücken) inmitten von Trennungsgerüchten bei einem abendlichen Millenniums-Vortrag zum Thema „Die Frau als Bürgerin" im East Room des Weißen Hauses, 15. März 1999.

… mais que de nuits solitaires. Au milieu des rumeurs de séparation, les Clinton apparaissent ensemble mais dos à dos lors d'une des conférences du Millénaire sur le thème « Femmes et citoyennes », tenue dans la East Room de la Maison Blanche, le 15 mars 1999.

The historic handshake of Prime Minister Iitzhak Rabin of Israel (left) and the PLO chairman Yasser Arafat at the White House, 13 September 1993.

Der historische Händedruck zwischen Israels Premier Itzhak Rabin (links) und PLO-Führer Yassir Arafat vor dem Weißen Haus, 13. September 1993.

La poignée de main historique entre Iitzhak Rabin, le Premier ministre d'Israël (à gauche), et Yasser Arafat, le chef de l'OLP, à la Maison Blanche, le 13 septembre 1993.

JIM HOLLANDER/REUTERS/ARCHIVE PHOTOS

Hoping for peace. Iitzhak Rabin surveys the West Bank from the Allenby Bridge on the Israel-Jordan border, 6 January 1994. Israel and the PLO had agreed to restart talks to implement the Gaza-Jericho Accord.

Hoffnung auf Frieden. Itzhak Rabin begutachtet das Westufer von der Allenby-Brücke aus, an der israelisch-jordanischen Grenze, 6. Januar 1994. Israel und die PLO waren übereingekommen, die Verhandlungen über die Umsetzung des Gaza-Jericho-Abkommens wieder aufzunehmen.

Espoir de paix. Iitzhak Rabin observe la rive ouest du Jourdain depuis le pont Allenby, à la frontière israélo-jordanienne, le 6 janvier 1994. Israël et l'OLP s'étaient mis d'accord pour reprendre les discussions sur l'application de l'accord Gaza-Jéricho.

Preparing for war.
Benjamin Netanyahu
examines a laser-
sighted Tavor at the
Israeli Defence
Forces technology
base, Tel Aviv,
2 September 1997.

Kriegsvorbereitung.
Benjamin Netanjahu
inspiziert ein
lasergestütztes
Tavor-Gewehr im
technologischen
Zentrum der israeli-
schen Verteidigungs-
armee in Tel Aviv,
2. September 1997.

Préparation de
guerre. Benjamin
Netanyahu, en visite
à la base technolo-
gique des Forces de
défense d'Israël, près
de Tel-Aviv, examine
un fusil-mitrailleur
Tavor à visée laser,
le 2 septembre 1997.

EPA/PA

EPA/PA

Funeral of a king. (From left to right) President Clinton, Hosni Mubarak of
Egypt, Ali Abdullah Saleh of the Yemen, and the PLO leader Yasser Arafat at the
funeral of King Hussein of Jordan, Amman, 8 February 1999.

Beisetzung eines Königs. (Von links nach rechts) Präsident Clinton, Ägyptens
Präsident Hosni Mubarak, Jemens Staatsoberhaupt Ali Abdullah Saleh und
PLO-Führer Yassir Arafat beim Begräbnis von König Hussein von Jordanien in
Amman, am 8. Februar 1999.

Funérailles d'un roi. (De gauche à droite) Le président Clinton, Hosni Mubarak
d'Égypte, Ali Abdullah Saleh du Yemen et le chef de l'OLP Yasser Arafat aux
funérailles du roi Hussein de Jordanie à Amman, le 8 février 1999.

YANNIS BEHRAKIS/REUTERS/ARCHIVE PHOTOS

King at a funeral. King Hussein delivers the eulogy at the funeral of the Israeli Prime Minister Iitzhak Rabin, Jerusalem, 6 November 1995. Rabin had been assassinated – a direct result of the handshake with Arafat two years earlier.

König bei einer Beisetzung. König Hussein hält die Grabrede beim Begräbnis des israelischen Premierministers Itzhak Rabin in Jerusalem, 6. November 1995. Rabin fiel einem Attentat zum Opfer, das eine direkte Folge des zwei Jahre zurückliegenden Handschlags mit Arafat war.

Un roi aux funérailles. Le roi Hussein prononce à Jérusalem, le 6 novembre 1995, l'éloge funèbre du Premier ministre d'Israël Iitzhak Rabin, mort assassiné – conséquence directe de sa poignée de mains avec Arafat, deux ans plus tôt.

Have tent, will
travel... President
Hosni Mubarak of
Egypt (right) meets
Colonel Gaddafi of
Libya in the latter's
modest tent, Cairo,
6 March 1999.

Mit einem Zelt
auf Reisen ... Der
ägyptische Präsident
Hosni Mubarak
(rechts) trifft Libyens
Oberst Gaddafi in
dessen bescheide-
nem Zelt in Kairo,
6. März 1999.

Qui a sa tente,
voyage ... Le prési-
dent égyptien Hosni
Mubarak (à droite)
rencontre le colonel
Kadhafi au Caire,
le 6 mars 1999, sous
la modeste tente du
chef libyen.

(Opposite) Mother Theresa and Pope John Paul II meet at the Vatican, 20 May 1997. (Right) Sandra Tigica and Diana, Princess of Wales, Luanda, 14 January 1997.

(Gegenüberliegende Seite) Mutter Theresa und Papst Johannes Paul II. bei ihrem Treffen im Vatikan am 20. Mai 1997. (Rechts) Sandra Tigica und Diana, Prinzessin von Wales, in Luanda, 14. Januar 1997.

(Ci-contre) Rencontre entre mère Teresa et le pape Jean-Paul II au Vatican, le 20 mai 1997. (À droite) Sandra Tigica et Diana, princesse de Galles, à Luanda, le 14 janvier 1997.

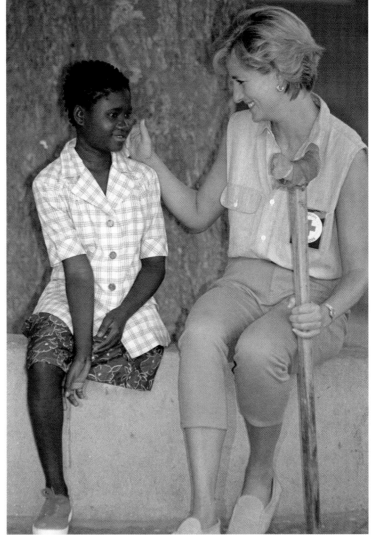

JOHN STILLWELL/PA

Boris steps out… President Yeltsin puts the dance floor to the test during an election rally, Rostov, Russia, 10 June 1996.

Boris hält Schritt … Während einer Wahl-veranstaltung im russischen Rostow stellt Präsident Jelzin den Tanzboden auf die Probe, 10. Juni 1996.

Boris se lance … Le président Eltsine met l'estrade à l'épreuve lors de sa tournée électorale à Rostov (Russie), le 10 juin 1996.

Full glasses, high hopes.
The Kohls and the
Yeltsins dine together in
splendour at Deides-
heimer Hof, 1994.

Volle Gläser, große
Hoffnungen. Die
Ehepaare Kohl und
Jelzin beim Diner im
prachtvollen Deides-
heimer Hof, 1994.

Un toast à l'espoir.
Les Kohl et les Eltsine
dînent ensemble dans
le cadre luxueux du
Deidesheimer Hof,
en 1994.

Off with the old… (opposite) Chancellor Helmut Kohl of Germany on holiday in Rio de Janeiro, 1991. (Above)… and on with the new. Gerhard Schröder, his successor as leader of the new united Germany, gets down to work in 1998.

Der Alte geht … (Gegenüberliegende Seite) Bundeskanzler Helmut Kohl während seines Urlaubs in Rio de Janeiro, 1991. (Oben) … der Neue kommt: Gerhard Schröder, sein Nachfolger als Kanzler des wieder vereinigten Deutschlands, macht sich an die Arbeit, 1998.

Dehors l'ancien… (Ci-contre) Le chancelier allemand Helmut Kohl, en vacances à Rio de Janeiro en 1991. (Ci-dessus) … et bienvenue au jeune. Gerhard Schröder, son successeur à la tête de la nouvelle Allemagne réunifiée, partant au travail en 1998.

Prime Minister
Margaret Thatcher
leaves Downing
Street for the
last time,
21 November 1990.
The 1980s had
finally come to an
end in Britain.

Premierministerin
Margaret Thatcher
verlässt am
21. November 1990
zum letzten Mal die
Downing Street.
Damit waren die
achtziger Jahre in
Großbritannien
endgültig vorbei.

Le Premier ministre
britannique Marga-
ret Thatcher quitte
pour la dernière fois
Downing Street, le
21 novembre 1990.
Cela marque la fin
définitive des années
quatre-vingt.

ADAM BUTLER/PA

New man, old methods. John Major takes the battle out on to the streets
of Luton in the run-up to the General Election, 3 March 1992. It was a
surprising, and ultimately successful, tactic.

Neuer Mann, alte Methoden. John Major als Wahlkämpfer in den
Straßen von Luton im Vorfeld der Wahlen zum Unterhaus, 3. März 1992.
Eine überraschende – und letztendlich erfolgreiche – Taktik.

À homme nouveau, vieilles méthodes. John Major mène personnelle-
ment le combat dans les rues de Luton lors de la campagne législative
britannique, le 3 mars 1992. Cette tactique surprenante se révéla
finalement payante.

New man, old problems. Tony Blair, Prime Minister of Britain, talks to Kosovar Albanian refugees, Blace, near Skopje, 3 May 1999. He was on a one-day visit to British soldiers serving with NATO forces.

Neuer Mann, alte Probleme. Der britische Premierminister Tony Blair im Gespräch mit albanischen Flüchtlingen aus dem Kosovo in Blace bei Skopje, 3. Mai 1999. Blair befand sich auf einem eintägigen Besuch bei britischen NATO-Soldaten.

À homme nouveau, vieux problèmes. Tony Blair, Premier ministre de Grande-Bretagne, parle avec des réfugiés Kosovar d'origine albanaise à Blace, près de Skopje, le 3 mai 1999. Il faisait une visite d'une journée aux soldats britanniques servant dans les forces de l'OTAN.

2. Conflict
Konflikte
Les conflits

A distraught boy at the funeral of his father. A Croatian policeman, he had been killed in an ambush during the fighting that followed the Croatian declaration of independence in June 1991.

Ein verzweifelter Junge bei der Beerdigung seines Vaters. Während der Kämpfe im Anschluss an die kroatische Unabhängigkeitserklärung im Juni 1991 wurde der kroatische Polizist in einem Hinterhalt getötet.

Un petit garçon désespéré à l'enterrement de son père, un policier croate, tué dans une embuscade lors des combats qui suivirent la déclaration d'indépendance de la Croatie en juin 1991.

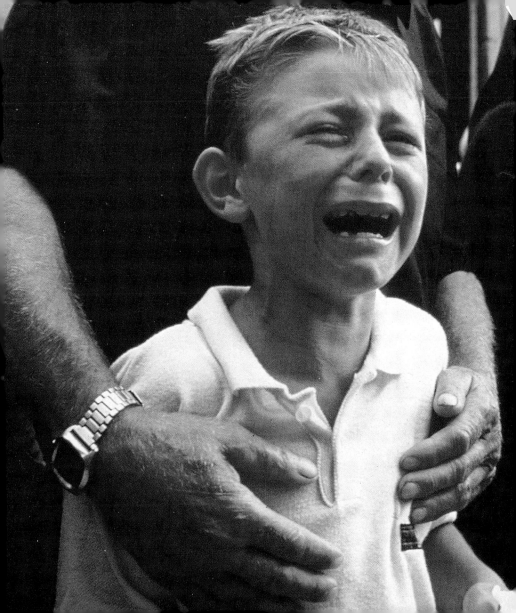

2. Conflict
Konflikte
Les conflits

There had been brave attempts to secure world peace ever since the slaughter of the First World War. Pacifists and politicians had looked to the League of Nations and the United Nations to set up an enforceable code of international law. Protesters had marched through the major cities of the world, calling for an end to nuclear weapons and for 'jaw-jaw' rather than 'war-war' as a means of settling disputes. And yet, more people died on the battlefield in the 20th century than in any other. War still dominated its last few years – in Asia, Africa, the Middle East, Central America and Europe.

Some of the conflicts were local affairs, armed struggles for the control of a country, a region, a neighbourhood. Others, like the Gulf War of 1991, featured the biggest players on the planet. War became a perverted kind of televised sport, a nightly serial for all to see in the comfort of their own homes. At whatever level they were fought, the wars seemed to prove that advances in the destructive power and sophistication of modern weaponry had not been tempered by advances in humanity or mercy. The second oldest sin in the Bible had reached potentially apocalyptic proportions.

Seit dem Gemetzel des Ersten Weltkrieges gab es mutige Versuche, den Weltfrieden zu sichern. Pazifisten und Politiker haben den Völkerbund und die Vereinten Nationen gedrängt, einen verbindlichen internationalen Gesetzes-Kodex zu entwerfen. Demonstranten zogen durch die Metropolen und setzten sich für die Abschaffung der Atomwaffen ein. Konflikte sollten mit Worten und nicht mit Waffen gelöst werden, so ihre Forderung. Dennoch forderten die Schlachtfelder des 20. Jahrhunderts mehr Opfer als jede andere Epoche zuvor. Kriege – in Asien, Afrika, im Nahen Osten, in Mittelamerika und in Europa – dominierten die letzten Jahre des vergangenen Jahrtausends.

Einige Auseinandersetzungen waren lokale Konflikte, bewaffnete Kämpfe um die Kontrolle eines Landes, einer Region, einer benachbarten Siedlung. Im Golfkrieg des Jahres 1991 traten die Weltmächte auf den Plan. Auf perverse Art und Weise wurde die kriegerische Auseinandersetzung zu einer Art Sportveranstaltung, zu einer Serie im Abendprogramm, die jeder Fernsehzuschauer im Schutz des eigenen Heims verfolgen konnte. Warum auch immer sie entbrannten – alle Kriege haben bewiesen, dass Menschlichkeit oder Barmherzigkeit mit der zunehmend zerstörerischen Kraft moderner Waffen nicht Schritt halten. Die zweitälteste Sünde des Alten Testamtents hat potenziell apokalyptische Ausmaße erreicht.

Il y avait eu de courageuses tentatives pour assurer la paix du monde depuis les massacres de la Première Guerre mondiale. Pacifistes et politiciens s'étaient tournés vers la Société des Nations puis les Nations Unies pour définir un code international vraiment applicable. Des manifestants avaient défilé dans les grandes capitales du monde, réclamant la fin de l'utilisation des armes nucléaires et le « bla-bla » plutôt que la « guéguerre » comme moyen de régler les différends. Et pourtant, plus d'hommes périrent sur les champs de bataille du XXᵉ siècle que dans tout autre. La guerre grondait encore en Asie, en Afrique, au Moyen-Orient, en Amérique centrale et en Europe.

Certains conflits étaient des problèmes locaux, des luttes armées pour le contrôle d'un pays, d'une région, d'une terre voisine. D'autres, comme la guerre du Golfe en 1991, mirent en scène les plus grands acteurs de la planète. La guerre devint une émission de sport télévisé perverti, une série diffusée en nocturne que tous pouvaient regarder dans le confort de leur maison. Quelle que soit leur importance, ces guerres semblaient démontrer que les progrès de l'armement moderne en termes de puissance destructrice et de sophistication n'avaient pas leur équivalent en humanité et en miséricorde. Le second plus ancien péché de la Bible avait atteint des proportions potentiellement apocalyptiques.

US marines in
action at the height
of Operation
Desert Storm during
the Gulf War,
26 February 1991.

Amerikanische
Marinesoldaten im
Einsatz auf dem
Höhepunkt der
„Operation Wüsten-
sturm" während des
Golfkrieges,
26. Februar 1991.

Des US marines
en action au plus
fort de l'opération
Tempête du Désert,
pendant la guerre
du Golfe, le
26 février 1991.

NOEL QUIDU/LIAISON AGENCY

An Iraqi civilian examines damage to a bunker inflicted by an Allied bombing raid on Baghdad, 22 February 1991. The so-called 'smart' bombs of the Allies had an embarrassing habit of hitting the wrong targets.

Ein irakischer Zivilist begutachtet einen zerstörten Bunker, der während eines Bombenangriffs der Alliierten auf Bagdad getroffen wurde, 22. Februar 1991. Die so genannten „intelligenten" Bomben der Alliierten hatten die peinliche Eigenschaft, mitunter die falschen Ziele zu treffen.

Un civil irakien examine les dégâts infligés à un bunker après un bombardement allié sur Bagdad, le 22 février 1991. Les bombes prétendument « intelligentes » des Alliés avaient pris l'ennuyeuse habitude de frapper les mauvaises cibles.

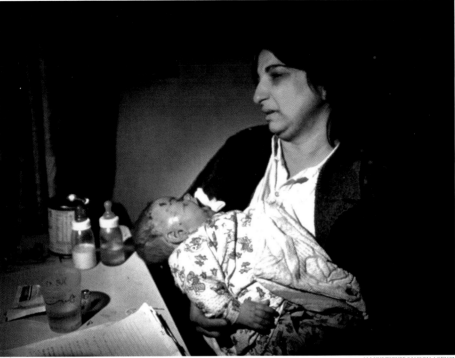

An Iraqi woman seeks to comfort her baby, wounded during a bomb attack on Baghdad, 7 February 1991. By the end of the war, some 250 Allied troops and more than 150,000 Iraqis had been killed.

Eine irakische Frau versucht ihr Baby zu trösten, das während eines Bombenangriffs auf Bagdad am 7. Februar 1991 verletzt wurde. Im Golfkrieg wurden über 150 000 Iraker getötet, die Alliierten verloren rund 250 Soldaten.

Une Irakienne cherche à réconforter son enfant, blessé pendant un bombardement sur Bagdad, le 7 février 1991. À la fin de la guerre, on allait compter près de 250 soldats alliés et plus de 150 000 Irakiens tués.

GILLES BASSIGNAC/LIAISON AGENCY

Iraq fights back. The remains of an Iraqi Scud missile intercepted by
US Patriot missiles over Riyadh, Saudi Arabia, 22 January 1991.
The war was just six days old and had five more weeks to run.

Der Irak schlägt zurück. Die Überreste einer Scud-Rakete, die von amerikanischen Patriot-Raketen über Riad, Saudi-Arabien, abgeschossen wurde,
22. Januar 1991. Der Krieg war gerade sechs Tage alt und sollte noch
fünf Wochen andauern.

L'Irak riposte. Les restes d'un Scud irakien intercepté par les missiles Patriot
américains au-dessus de Riyad (Arabie Saoudite), le 22 janvier 1991. La guerre
avait commencé depuis à peine six jours et devait durer cinq semaines encore.

ESAÏAS BAITEL/LIAISON AGENCY

An Iraqi Scud inflicts heavy damage on Tel Aviv, Israel, 22 January 1991.
Such photographs helped the Allies gain the high moral ground during
the propaganda struggle.

Am selben Tag detoniert eine irakische Scud in Tel Aviv, Israel,
und verursacht großen Schaden. Solche Fotos halfen den Alliierten,
die moralische Rechtfertigung des Krieges propagandistisch zu
untermauern.

Un Scud irakien a provoqué d'importants dégâts à Tel Aviv (Israël), le
22 janvier 1991. Des photographies comme celles-ci ont permis aux
Alliés de remporter une victoire morale dans la lutte des propagandes.

(Above and opposite) Contrasting portraits of the Gulf War.
(Above) American High Command: (from left to right) General Colin
Powell and General 'Stormin'' Norman Schwarzkopf.

(Oben und gegenüberliegende Seite) Kontrastierende Fotos des
Golfkrieges. (Oben, von links nach rechts) Der amerikanische
Oberbefehlshaber General Colin Powell und General Norman
Schwarzkopf, der „Wüstenstürmer".

(Ci-dessus et ci-contre) Des images contrastées de la guerre du Golfe.
(Ci-dessus, de gauche à droite) Le haut commandement américain :
les généraux Colin Powell et « Stormin' » Norman Schwarzkopf.

DENNIS BRACK/BLACK STAR/COLORIFIC!

The highway of death: the Baghdad–Basra road after an American bombing raid, 28 February 1991. Iraqi losses were at their heaviest in the last few days of the war, after their defence system had been all but obliterated.

Der Highway des Todes: Die Straße zwischen Bagdad und Basra nach einem Luftangriff der Amerikaner, 28. Februar 1991. Die Verluste der Iraker waren in den letzten Tagen des Krieges am größten, nachdem ihr Verteidigungssystem so gut wie ausgeschaltet war.

L'autoroute de la mort : la route Bagdad-Bassora après un bombardement américain, le 28 février 1991. Les pertes de l'Irak furent très lourdes en quelques jours de guerre à cause de l'anéantissement complet de son système de défense.

L VAN DER STOCKT/LIAISON AGENCY

Prayers of the faithful. Saudi soldiers, part of the Arab coalition forces ranged against Iraq, at prayer in the desert, 4 September 1990. The force was assembled after Saddam Hussein seized Kuwait.

Die Gebete der Gläubigen. Saudische Soldaten – ein Teil der arabischen Koalitions-Streitkräfte, die gegen den Irak aufgestellt worden waren – beten in der Wüste, 4. September 1990. Die Streitkräfte wurden zusammengestellt, nachdem Saddam Hussein in Kuwait einmarschiert war.

La prière des fidèles. Des soldats saoudiens, appartenant à la coalition arabe contre l'Irak, prient dans le désert, le 4 septembre 1990. Ces forces furent réunies après l'invasion du Koweit par Saddam Hussein.

GILLES SAUSSIER/LIAISON AGENCY

Prey of the Allies. Troops of the Arab coalition confront three Iraqi soldiers taken prisoner during the liberation of Kuwait, 28 February 1991. Tens of thousands of Iraqis were captured during the operation.

Die Beute der Alliierten. Truppen der arabischen Koalition halten drei irakische Soldaten in Schach, die bei der Befreiung Kuwaits am 28. Februar 1991 festgenommen wurden. Zehntausende Irakis wurden während der Operation gefangen genommen.

La proie des Alliés. Les troupes de la coalition arabe font face à trois soldats irakiens faits prisonniers lors de la libération du Koweit, le 28 février 1991. Des dizaines de milliers d'Irakiens furent ainsi capturés au cours de l'opération.

MARC DEVILLE/LIAISON AGENCY

The war against the Kurds. A section of a vast Kurdish refugee encampment at Silopi transit camp, Turkey, 17 April 1991. With the end of the Gulf War, Saddam Hussein was free to turn his wrath on opponents within Iraq's borders.

Der Krieg gegen die Kurden. Ein Teil des riesigen kurdischen Flüchtlings-Camps im Übergangslager von Silopi, Türkei, 17. April 1991. Nach dem Golfkrieg konnte Saddam Hussein seinen Zorn ungestört auf Gegner im Irak richten.

La guerre contre les Kurdes. Une partie du vaste camp de transit des réfugiés kurdes à Silopi, en Turquie, le 17 avril 1991. La guerre du Golfe terminée, Saddam Hussein était libre de retourner sa colère sur les populations à l'intérieur de ses frontières.

One of the hundreds of victims severely burnt during poison gas attacks by Iraqi troops in Kurdistan, 1994.

Ein Opfer unter hundert anderen, die 1994 während eines Giftgas-Angriffs irakischer Truppen in Kurdistan schwer verbrannt wurden.

Une des nombreuses victimes gravement brûlées lors d'une attaque aux gaz des troupes irakiennes au Kurdistan, en 1994.

GÜNTHER MENN/FOCUS/COLORIFIC!

A Kurdish woman
holds aloft a portrait
of the PKK leader
Abdullah Öcalan at
a protest meeting
in The Hague,
16 February 1999.

Eine kurdische Frau
hält bei einer Pro-
testversammlung in
Den Haag ein Bild
des PKK-Führers
Abdullah Öcalan
in die Höhe,
16. Februar 1999.

Une Kurde brandit
un portrait du leader
du PKK, Abdullah
Öcalan, lors d'une
manifestation à
la Haye,
le 16 février 1999.

JERRY LAMPEN/REUTERS/ARCHIVE PHOTOS

SRYROS TSAKIRIS/REUTERS/ARCHIVE PHOTOS

In an attempt to thwart attempts by Greek police to break up a Kurdish protest outside the Greek Parliament building in Athens, 15 February 1999, two of the protesters set light to themselves.

Zwei Kurden setzten sich in Brand, um zu verhindern, dass die griechische Polizei eine kurdische Demonstration vor dem Parlamentsgebäude in Athen auflöst, 15. Februar 1999.

Deux manifestants s'immolent par le feu pour tenter de résister à la dispersion de la manifestation kurde par la police grecque devant le parlement d'Athènes, le 15 février 1999.

CHRISTOPHER MORRIS/BLACK STAR/COLORIFIC!

Armed with riot shield and rubber truncheon wrested from the police, a Russian protester adds passion to an anti-Yeltsin demonstration in front of the White House in Moscow, 3 October 1993.

Bewaffnet mit Schutzschild und Gummiknüppel, die er einem Polizisten abgenommen hat, nimmt ein russischer Demonstrant lautstark an einer Anti-Jelzin-Kundgebung vor dem Weißen Haus in Moskau teil, 3. Oktober 1993.

Un manifestant russe, armé d'un bouclier anti-émeute et d'une matraque de caoutchouc arrachés à un policier, enflamme une manifestation anti-Eltsine devant la Maison Blanche de Moscou, le 3 octobre 1993.

A civilian killed during the demonstration. Yeltsin's announcement that he was suspending the Russian Parliament intensified the struggle between pro- and anti-reform groups. The following morning, Yeltsin ordered tanks to fire on the rebels.

Ein Zivilist, der während einer Demonstration getötet wurde. Jelzins Ankündigung, das russische Parlament aufzulösen, heizte den Kampf zwischen Pro- und Anti-Reformgruppen an. Am folgenden Morgen befahl Jelzin den Panzerfahrern, auf die Rebellen zu schießen.

Un civil tué lors de la manifestation. L'annonce par Eltsine qu'il dissolvait le Parlement russe intensifia la lutte entre les groupes pro- et anti-réformes. Le lendemain, Eltsine ordonnait aux chars de tirer sur les rebelles.

A further chapter of Russian woe. A Chechen sniper takes aim in the ruins of Grozny, 1996.

Ein weiteres Kapitel russischen Leids. Ein tschetschenischer Scharfschütze nimmt in den Ruinen von Grozny sein Ziel ins Visier, 1996.

Un autre chapitre du malheur russe.
Un sniper tchétchène en position dans les ruines de Grozny, en 1996.

CHRISTOPHER MORRIS/BLACK STAR/COLORIFIC!

Chechen dead. A Russian soldier strides past a ditch littered with victims of the fighting in the area around Grozny, 1995. The war had begun to pick up towards the end of 1994; by February 1995, Grozny was little more than a ghost town.

Der tschetschenische Tod. Ein russischer Soldat geht an einem Graben vorbei, der angefüllt ist mit den Opfern der Kämpfe um Grozny, 1995. Der Krieg begann Ende 1994, im Februar 1995 war Grozny nur noch eine Geisterstadt.

Morts tchétchènes. Un soldat russe longe un fossé où s'entassent les victimes des combats menés en 1995 dans la région de Grozny. La guerre avait repris fin 1994 et, dès février 1995, Grozny n'était guère plus qu'une ville fantôme.

Russian dead. Two days before these paratroopers were killed by grenade fire the Russian photographer Vladamir Velengurin had been chatting with them. 'A couple of minutes after I took this frame their bodies were taken away by helicopter.'

Der russische Tod. Zwei Tage bevor diese Fallschirmjäger in einem Granatenhagel getötet wurden, hatte sich der russische Fotograf Vladamir Velengurin noch mit ihnen unterhalten. „Ein paar Minuten, nachdem ich diese Aufnahme gemacht habe, wurden ihre Leichen mit Helikoptern abtransportiert."

Morts russes. Le photographe russe Vladamir Velengurin avait discuté deux jours avant avec ces parachutistes, décimés par un tir de grenades : « Quelques minutes après cette photo, leurs corps étaient emportés par hélicoptère. »

CHRISTOPHER MORRIS/BLACK STAR/COLORIFIC!

'Welcome to Sarajevo' says the slogan on the bullet-spattered wall,
19 May 1995. The dismemberment of Yugoslavia was one of the
bitterest and most drawn-out events of the 1990s.

„Willkommen in Sarajevo" lautet der Slogan auf der mit Einschüssen
übersäten Wand, 19. Mai 1995. Die Zersplitterung Jugoslawiens gehörte
zu den der bittersten und langwierigsten Krisen der neunziger Jahre.

« Bienvenue à Sarajevo » dit le slogan inscrit sur ce mur constellé
d'impact de balles, le 19 mai 1995. Le démembrement de la Yougoslavie
fut l'un des événements les plus violents et les plus longs des années
quatre-vingt-dix.

CHRISTOPHER MORRIS/BLACK STAR/COLORIFIC!

The 'spark that set the world ablaze' returns to Sarajevo, 1992. After EC recognition of Croatia and Slovenia in January 1992, Bosnia-Herzegovina declared itself independent and an ethnic powder keg exploded in the Balkans.

Der „Funke, der die Welt in Flammen setzte" kehrt nach Sarajevo zurück, 1992. Nachdem die Europäische Gemeinschaft im Jahre 1992 die Staaten Kroatien und Slowenien anerkannte, erklärte auch Bosnien-Herzegowina seine Unabhängigkeit, und ein ethnisches Pulverfass explodierte auf dem Balkan.

« L'étincelle qui embrase le monde » tombe sur Sarajevo en 1992. En déclarant également son indépendance après la reconnaissance de la Croatie et de la Slovénie par la Communauté européenne en janvier 1992, la Bosnie-Herzégovine provoque l'explosion de la poudrière ethnique des Balkans.

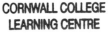

CHRISTOPHER MORRIS/BLACK STAR/COLORIFIC!

Croatian troops advance on Serb positions in Vukovar, October 1991.
The photographer accompanied the soldiers until they were within close
to 50 yards of the enemy.

Kroatische Truppen nähern sich einem serbischen Posten in Vukovar, Oktober 1991.
Der Fotograf begleitete die Soldaten bis auf etwa 50 Meter Entfernung von den Serben.

Les troupes croates avancent sur les positions serbes à Vukovar, en octobre 1991.
Le photographe a accompagné les soldats jusqu'à une cinquantaine de mètres des
positions ennemies.

The remains of Vukovar, November 1991. Of the original 81,000 inhabitants, only 5,000 remained. Here, some of the survivors flee the city.

Die Überreste von Vukovar im November 1991. Von den ursprünglich 81 000 Bewohnern waren nur noch 5000 geblieben. Hier fliehen einige der Überlebenden aus der Stadt.

Les ruines de Vukovar en novembre 1991. Il ne restait que 5000 habitants sur les 81 000 que comptait la ville. Comme ceux-ci, beaucoup quittèrent la ville.

CHRISTOPHER MORRIS/BLACK STAR/COLORIFIC!

Where words fail. The bodies of slaughtered
Croatian civilians – old and young – waiting to be
buried, Vukovar, November 1991.

Wo Worte versagen. Die Leichen niedergemetzelter
kroatischer Zivilisten – alte und junge –, bevor sie
beigesetzt wurden. Vukovar, November 1991.

Au-delà des mots. Les corps massacrés de ces civils
croates – jeunes et vieux – attendent d'être enterrés
à Vukovar, en novembre 1991.

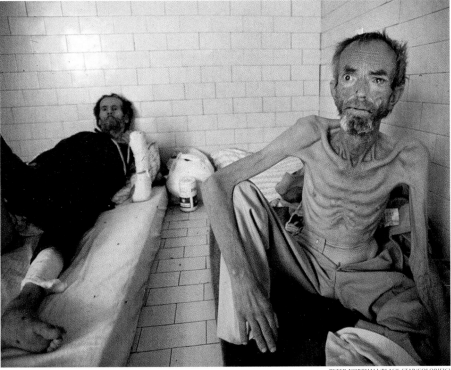

The stark reality of 'ethnic cleansing' – Muslim refugees in a camp near Puropolje, Yugoslavia. Hundreds of thousands lost their homes. Tens of thousands were killed. The search to find the thousands still missing continues.

Die harte Realität der „ethnischen Säuberung" – das muslimische Flüchtlingslager nahe Puropolje, Jugoslawien. Hunderttausende verloren ihr Zuhause. Zehntausende wurden getötet. Die Suche nach den Tausenden, die noch immer vermisst werden, dauert an.

La dure réalité de la « purification ethnique » : des réfugiés musulmans dans un camp près de Puropolje, en Yougoslavie. Des centaines de milliers perdirent leur maison. Des dizaines de milliers furent tués. Et l'on recherche encore les milliers qui sont toujours disparus.

EPA/PA

The helmet belongs to an American soldier of the 26th Marine Expeditionary Unit. The names are those of Kosovan children. The picture was taken during a lunch in Gniljane (near Pristina) marking America's Independence Day, 4 July 1999.

Diesen Helm eines amerikanischen Soldaten der 26. Marine-Expeditionseinheit zieren die Namen von Kindern aus dem Kosovo. Das Bild wurde bei einem Mittagessen zur Feier des amerikanischen Unabhängigkeitstags, am 4. Juli 1999, in Gniljane nahe Pristina aufgenommen.

Ce casque appartient à un soldat américain de la 26ᵉ Marine Expeditionary Unit. Les noms sont ceux d'enfants du Kosovo. Cette photographie a été prise le 4 juillet 1999 lors d'un déjeuner à Gniljane (près de Pristina) commémorant le jour de l'Indépendance des États-Unis.

TYLER HICKS/LIAISON AGENCY

NATO air strikes set fire to the city of Pristina, Kosovo, 25 March 1999.
A year later, NATO military and political leaders visited Pristina to mark
the event.

Nato-Luftangriffe setzen die Innenstadt Pristinas am 25. März 1999 in
Flammen. Ein Jahr später besuchten Nato-Militärs und führende Politiker
Pristina, um dieses Tages zu gedenken.

Les frappes aériennes de l'OTAN mettent le feu à Pristina, au Kosovo,
le 25 mars 1999. Un an plus tard, les chefs politiques et militaires de
l'OTAN venaient sur les lieux marquer l'événement.

DAVID BRAUCHLI/LIAISON AGENCY

'…women must weep…' An Albanian refugee from Kosovo comforts a small girl in the village school at Bob, 30 miles south of Pristina, 2 March 1999. Fighting between Serbs and the KLA had forced them to leave their homes.

„… Frauen müssen weinen …" Ein albanischer Flüchtling aus dem Kosovo tröstet ein kleines Mädchen in der Schule des Ortes Bob, 50 Kilometer südlich von Pristina, 2. März 1999. Die Kämpfe zwischen den Serben und der Kosovo-Befreiungsarmee UCK zwangen sie, ihre Häuser zu verlassen.

« … si les femmes doivent pleurer … » Une réfugiée albanaise du Kosovo réconforte une petite fille de l'école du village de Bob, à 50 kilomètres au sud de Pristina, le 2 mars 1999. Les combats entre Serbes et forces de l'ALK les ont contraintes à quitter leur maison.

THOMAS SJOERUP/BLACK STAR/COLORIFIC!

'…must men kill and die?' Members of the Kosovo Liberation Army hurry through the streets of Svrg during a running battle with security forces, 14 March 1999.

„… Müssen Männer töten und sterben?" Mitglieder der UCK rennen während eines Gefechts mit Sicherheits-streitkräften durch die Straßen von Svrg, 14. März 1999.

« … les hommes doivent-ils tuer et mourir ? » Des membres de l'Armée de Libération du Kosovo, en lutte contre les forces de sécurité, défilent dans les rues de Svrg, le 14 mars 1999.

Thousands of
Kosovar refugees
gather in a camp
near Kukes and the
border with Kosovo,
April 1999.

Tausende Flücht-
linge aus dem
Kosovo in einem
Lager nahe Kukes
an der Grenze zum
Kosovo, April 1999.

Des milliers de
réfugiés kosovars
sont rassemblés
dans un camp
proche de Kukes,
à la frontière
du Kosovo,
en avril 1999.

CORINNE DUFKA/REUTERS/ARCHIVE PHOTOS

Like a river in flood, refugees from the town of Uvira stream past a guard near Nyangezi, Zaire, 23 October 1996. They were fleeing from fighting between Zairean troops and Bangamulenge Tutsi rebels.

Der Flüchtlingsstrom: Einwohner der Stadt Uvira gehen nahe Nyangezi, Zaire, an einer Wache vorbei, 23. Oktober 1996. Sie fliehen vor den Kämpfen zwischen zairischen Truppen und Tutsi-Rebellen aus Bangamulenge.

Des réfugiés de la ville d'Uvira passent comme un fleuve en crue devant un garde près de Nyangezi, au Zaïre, le 23 octobre 1996. Ils fuyaient les combats entre les troupes zaïroises et les rebelles Tutsi Bangamulenge.

Under the protection
of French soldiers,
children play at the
Niashishi camp,
southern Rwanda,
30 June 1994.

Unter dem Schutz
französischer
Soldaten spielen
diese Kinder im
Niashishi-Camp im
Süden Ruandas,
30. Juni 1994.

Des enfants jouent
sous la protection
de soldats français
au camp de Nia-
shishi, dans le sud
du Rwanda,
le 30 juin 1994.

PASCAL GUYOT/EPA/PA

Offering protection. A local man shelters a child while a French soldier mounts guard, Brazzaville, Congo, 11 June 1997.

Schutz. Dieser Einwohner Brazzavilles beschützt ein Kind, während ein französischer Soldat Wache hält, Brazzaville, Kongo, 11. Juni 1997.

Protéger. Un Congolais protège un enfant tandis qu'un soldat français monte la garde à Brazzaville (Congo), le 11 juin 1997.

DAN ELDON/REUTERS/ARCHIVE PHOTOS

Threatening action. US marine Staff Sergeant Ken Haughen aims the pistol he has just taken from this 15-year-old Somali at the boy's head, February 1993. The incident took place on Mogadishu's 'green line'.

Bedrohung. Ken Haughen, Stabsfeldwebel der US-Marine, richtet die Pistole auf einen 15-jährigen Somali. Haughen hatte dem Jungen die Waffe soeben abgenommen, Februar 1993. Die Szene ereignete sich an der „grünen Linie" in Mogadischu.

Menacer. Le sergent-chef Ken Haughen, des US Marines, menace un jeune Somalien de quinze ans avec le pistolet qu'il vient de lui prendre, en février 1993. L'incident a lieu sur la « ligne verte » de Mogadiscio.

CORINNE DUFKA/REUTERS/ARCHIVE PHOTOS

Monrovia, Liberia, 8 May 1996. The story is best told in the words of the photographer, 'The nameless man had crept out of his house in search of something to eat…[he was] caught by a patrol of armed NPFL men…'

Monrovia, Liberia, 8. Mai 1996. Die Geschichte dieser Aufnahmen in den Worten der Fotografin: „Der unbekannte Mann kam aus seinem Haus gekrochen, auf der Suche nach etwas Essbarem … [als er] von einem Mitglied der Nationalen Befreiungsarmee Liberias (NPFL) gestellt wurde …"

Monrovia, Liberia, 8 mai 1996. La photographe raconte : « Cet inconnu est sorti de sa maison pour chercher quelque chose à manger … [lorsqu'il fut] aperçu par les hommes d'une patrouille du NPFL … ».

CORINNE DUFKA/REUTERS/ARCHIVE PHOTOS

'…within eight minutes he had been told to run, shot in the back, then dragged down the street and stripped down to his socks and underwear… the boss man finished him off.' At home a family waited for him to return with the food he never found.

„… innerhalb von acht Minuten befahl man ihm zu rennen, schoss ihm in den Rücken, schleifte ihn die Straße hinab und zog ihn bis auf Unterwäsche und Strümpfe aus … schließlich kam der Anführer der Truppe und gab ihm den Rest." Zu Hause wartete eine Familie auf ihn und das Essen, das er nie auftrieb.

« … qui, en l'espace de huit minutes, l'obligèrent à courir, lui tirèrent dans le dos, puis le traînèrent dans la rue pour le dépouiller de ses chaussettes et de ses sous-vêtements … Leur chef l'acheva lui-même ». Dans une maison, une famille attend son retour avec la nourriture qu'il n'a jamais trouvée.

GEORGE MULALA/REUTERS/ARCHIVE PHOTOS

Survivors of the bombing of the US Embassy, Nairobi, Kenya, 7 August 1999. Two hundred and fifty people were killed and 5,000 injured.

Überlebende des Bombenanschlags auf die amerikanische Botschaft von Nairobi, Kenia, 7. August 1999. 250 Menschen wurden getötet, über 5000 verletzt.

Des survivants du bombardement de l'ambassade américaine à Nairobi, au Kenya, le 7 août 1999. Deux cent cinquante personnes furent tuées et 5000 blessées.

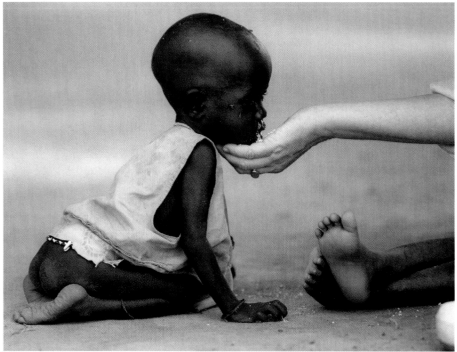

ERIC FEFERBERG/EPA/PA

A lull in the fighting. Food supplied by humanitarian aid workers is given
to a baby in Akon, Bar-el-Ghazal province, Sudan, 10 October 1998.
A three-month ceasefire had been negotiated in the civil war.

Gefechtspause. Ein Mitglied einer humanitären Hilfsorganisation füttert dieses
Baby in Akon, Provinz Bar-el-Ghazal im Sudan, 10. Oktober 1998. Inmitten
des Bürgerkrieges wurde ein dreimonatiger Waffenstillstand vereinbart.

Une accalmie dans les combats. Un bébé bénéficie de la nourriture fournie
par les équipes d'aide humanitaire à Akon, dans la province soudanaise de
Bar-el-Ghazal, le 10 octobre 1998. Un cessez-le-feu de trois mois avait été
négocié pendant la guerre civile.

EPA/PA

Back to business. Members of the Sudanese People's Liberation Army undergo training in a 'liberated zone', eastern Sudan, 10 November 1999. The war against the Islamic Government in Khartoum had already lasted ten years.

Zurück zu den Waffen. Mitglieder der sudanesischen Volksbefreiungsarmee absolvieren in einer „befreiten Zone" im Osten des Landes eine Trainingseinheit, 10. November 1999. Zu diesem Zeitpunkt dauerte der Krieg gegen die islamische Regierung von Khartoum bereits zehn Jahre an.

Le travail reprend. Des membres de l'Armée de Libération du Peuple soudanais à l'entraînement dans une « zone libérée » du Soudan oriental, le 10 novembre 1999. La guerre contre le gouvernement islamique de Khartoum durait déjà depuis dix ans.

South Africans take
cover during an
incident between
UDM and ANC
supporters in the
Magoda township,
Richmond,
24 January 1999.

Während eines
Gefechts zwischen
Anhängern der UDM
und des ANC gehen
südafrikanische Zivi-
listen in Deckung,
Magoda Township,
Richmond,
24. Januar 1999.

Des Sud-Africains se
mettent à couvert
pendant un incident
entre partisans de
l'UDM et de l'ANC
dans le township
de Magoda,
à Richmond,
le 24 janvier 1999.

DAOUD MIZRAHI/EPA/PA

Israeli troops arrest a Palestinian in the town of Hebron, 3 June 1999. The youth had been taking part in a protest against Jewish settlement programmes in Jerusalem and the Palestinian territories.

In Hebron nehmen israelische Einheiten einen Palästinenser fest, 3. Juni 1999. Der junge Mann hatte an einer Demonstration gegen die israelische Siedlungspolitik in Jerusalem und den Palästinensergebieten teilgenommen.

Les troupes israéliennes arrêtent un Palestinien dans la ville d'Hébron, le 3 juin 1999. Le jeune homme avait pris part à une manifestation contre les programmes de colonisation juive à Jérusalem et dans les territoires palestiniens.

YISRAEL HADARI/REUTERS/ARCHIVE PHOTOS

An Israeli policeman (right) rushes to the aid of victims of a suicide bomb attack, Tel Aviv, 4 March 1996. Eleven people were killed and more than 100 injured. It was the fourth blast in nine days.

Ein israelischer Polizist (rechts) eilt den Opfern eines Selbstmord-Bombenanschlags in Tel Aviv zu Hilfe, 4. März 1996. 11 Menschen wurden getötet und mehr als 100 verletzt. Es war der vierte Anschlag innerhalb von neun Tagen.

Un policier israélien (à droite) se précipite pour secourir les victimes d'un attentat suicide à Tel Aviv, le 4 mars 1996. Onze personnes furent tuées et plus d'une centaine blessées. C'était le quatrième attentat en neuf jours.

BETH SHAMITZ/LIAISON AGENCY

Students file through the city morgue, Jakarta, November 1998. The bodies they sought to identify were those killed in anti-Government riots during the last months of President Suharto's authoritarian rule.

Studenten schreiten durch das Leichenschauhaus von Jakarta, November 1998. Sie wollen die Todesopfer der Aufstände gegen das autoritäre Regime Präsident Suhartos in den letzten Monaten seiner Herrschaft identifizieren.

Des étudiants défilent à la morgue de Jakarta, en novembre 1998. Les victimes qu'ils cherchent à identifier ont été tuées lors des émeutes antigouvernementales organisées pendant les derniers mois du règne autoritaire du président Suharto.

East Timorese
freedom fighters
stone an Indonesian
armed patrol, Dili,
12 October 1999.

Freiheitskämpfer in
Osttimor bewerfen
eine bewaffnete indo-
nesische Patrouille
mit Steinen. Dili,
12. Oktober 1999.

Les combattants
de la liberté du
Timor Oriental
lancent des pierres
sur une patrouille
militaire à Dili,
le 12 octobre 1999.

EPA/PA

3. New world order
Die neue Weltordnung
Nouvel ordre du monde

With a fetching touch of irony, a male visitor to the Latvian Nudist Colony in Saule seeks modesty behind the hammer and sickle, 10 June 1992. The Baltic republics had only recently achieved independence.

Ein reizender Hauch von Ironie. Dieser männliche Besucher der lettischen Nudistenkolonie von Saule bedeckt seine Blöße mit Hammer und Sichel, 10. Juni 1992. Die baltischen Republiken hatten erst kurz zuvor ihre Unabhängigkeit erlangt.

C'est avec une ironie charmante qu'un membre de la colonie nudiste lettone de Saule cache ses attributs derrière ceux du communisme soviétique – la faucille et le marteau, le 10 juin 1992. Les républiques baltes venaient d'obtenir leur indépendance.

3. New world order
Die neue Weltordnung
Nouvel ordre du monde

For more than seventy years the Communist east and the capitalist west had built their relationship on a basis of mutual loathing and mistrust. They stockpiled weapons against each other, launched networks of spies, frightened their respective populations into submission with tales of what the other side might do if it gained the upper hand. In so doing, they maintained a world order that was tightly, if fearfully, cohesive.

All this changed with the collapse of the Communist bloc in the early 1990s. The 'evil empire' that had so excited Ronald Reagan no longer existed. In its place was a vast land of opportunity whose economic potential excited Ronald McDonald. Consumerism replaced Communism. Coke added fizz to Muscovites' vodka. Sony invaded China. Shell invaded Poland. The accountant replaced the commissar. But, while east and west merged together, old federations fragmented. Ancient nations reappeared – Latvia, Estonia, Croatia and a dozen more. To its opponents, it was as though an antibiotic had at last been found to protect the world from socialism. The free market triumphed everywhere. No more five-year plans, no more state control, no more planned economies. After a century of struggle, capitalism had emerged triumphant, and the spirit of competition reigned supreme.

Über 70 Jahre basierte das Verhältnis zwischen dem kommunistischen Osten und dem kapitalistischen Westen auf gegenseitigem Misstrauen und Hass. Sie türmten Waffen gegeneinander auf, setzten Spionagenetze ein und sicherten sich den Gehorsam ihrer Völker mit Geschichten darüber, was die andere Seite täte, würde sie jemals die Oberhand gewinnen. Dadurch wurde eine straffe Weltordnung aufrechterhalten, die auf schreckliche Weise stabil war.

All das änderte sich mit dem Zusammenbruch des kommunistischen Blocks in den frühen neunziger Jahren. Das „Reich des Bösen", das Ronald Reagan so in Erregung versetzt hatte, existierte nicht mehr. An seine Stelle trat ein Schlaraffenland, dessen wirtschaftliches Potenzial nun Ronald McDonald in Erregung versetzte. Der Konsumismus ersetzte den Kommunismus. Coca-Cola brachte die Wodkas der Moskauer zum Prickeln. Sony marschierte in China ein. Shell besetzte Polen. Der Buchhalter ersetzte den Volkskommissar. Während Ost und West zusammenwuchsen, brachen alte Bündnisse zusammen. Vergessen geglaubte Nationen tauchten wieder auf – Lettland, Estland, Kroatien und ein Dutzend weitere. Für seine Gegner schien es, als sei endlich ein Antibiotikum entdeckt worden, das die Welt vor dem Sozialismus bewahrt. Der freie Markt triumphierte überall. Keine Fünfjahrespläne mehr, keine staatliche Kontrolle, keine Planwirtschaft. Aus einem Jahrhundert des Widerstreits ging der Kapitalismus als Sieger hervor und der Geist des Wettbewerbs übernahm die Herrschaft.

Pendant plus de 70 ans, l'Est communiste et l'Occident capitaliste avaient fondé leurs relations sur la base de la défiance et de la haine réciproques. Ils accumulèrent des armes l'un contre l'autre, lancèrent des réseaux d'espions, effrayèrent leurs populations respectives pour mieux les subjuguer en colportant des contes sur les intentions de l'autre s'il avait la suprématie. Par cela, ils maintenaient tous deux un ordre mondial étroitement, sinon anxieusement, cohésif.

Tout cela changea avec l'effondrement du bloc communiste au début des années 1990. « L'Empire du Mal » qui avait tant excité Ronald Reagan n'existait plus. On trouvait à la place un vaste champ d'opportunités, dont le potentiel économique excitait Ronald McDonald. Le consumérisme remplaçait le communisme. Le coca ajoutait du pétillant à la vodka des Moscovites. Sony envahissait la Chine. Shell envahissait la Pologne. Le comptable remplaçait le commissaire politique. Mais, tandis que l'Est et l'Ouest fusionnaient, les anciennes fédérations se fragmentaient. D'anciennes nations réapparaissaient : Lettonie, Estonie, Croatie et une douzaine d'autres. On pouvait croire qu'on avait trouvé un antibiotique pour protéger le monde du socialisme. Le libre marché triomphait partout. Plus de plans quinquennaux, plus de contrôle étatique, plus d'économie planifiée. Le capitalisme émergeait triomphalement d'un siècle de luttes, et l'esprit de concurrence régnait en maître.

Cheering Ethiopians
greet the fall of a
statue of Lenin,
two days after the
flight of President
Mengistu,
23 May 1991.

Begeisterte Äthio-
pier bejubeln den
Fall einer Lenin-
Statue zwei Tage
nach der Flucht
ihres Präsidenten
Mengistu,
23. Mai 1991.

Des Éthiopiens
en liesse saluent
la chute d'une
statue de Lénine,
deux jours après
la fuite du
président Mengistu,
le 23 mai 1991.

McFans… In the Chinese city of Shenzhen, the ubiquitous Ronald McDonald poses outside the first McDonald's restaurant in the country.

McFreunde … Der allgegenwärtige Ronald McDonald posiert in Shenzhen vor dem ersten McDonald's-Restaurant Chinas.

Fans de McDo … À Shenzhen, l'omniprésent Ronald McDonald pose devant le premier McDonald's de Chine.

McFoes... The ultra-nationalist Duma member Vladimir Zhirinovsky enquires about the meat content of a hamburger during an anti-McDonald's protest, Moscow, 27 August 1997.

McFeinde ... Während einer Anti-McDonald's-Demonstration in Moskau erkundigt sich das ultra-nationalistische Duma-Mitglied Wladimir Schirinowski öffentlich über den Fleischgehalt eines Hamburgers, 27. August 1997.

Ennemis de McDo ... Le député ultra-nationaliste de la Douma russe, Vladimir Zhirinovsky, s'inquiète du contenu d'un hamburger pendant une manifestation anti-McDonald's à Moscou, le 27 août 1997.

DAVID BRAUCHLI/LIAISON AGENCY

The 'real thing'.
A cyclist passes the
Coca-Cola bottling
plant in Hefei, Anhui
province, China,
26 February 1998.

„Probier was Neues"
... Ein Radfahrer
passiert die Coca-
Cola-Abfüllanlage
von Hefei in
der chinesischen
Provinz Anhui,
26. Februar 1998.

« Le goût du vrai ».
Un cycliste passe
devant l'usine
d'embouteillage
Coca-Cola de Hefei,
dans la province
chinoise du Anhui,
le 26 février 1998.

Never in the 'Thoughts of Chairman Mao' – a modern shopping complex in Beijing, China, 9 April 1998.

Gab es nicht in den „Worten des Vorsitzenden Mao": ein modernes Einkaufszentrum in Peking, China, 9. April 1998.

Ce complexe commercial moderne à Pékin, Chine, le 9 avril 1998, n'avait jamais été imaginé dans les « Pensées du président Mao ».

STEPHEN SHAVER/EPA/PA

A democratic future. East Germans get their
first taste of an election rally in Erfurt, East
Germany, 20 February 1990. Helmut Kohl
is the central figure.

Eine demokratische Zukunft. Die Ostdeutschen
bekommen einen ersten Eindruck vom Wahlkampf nach westlichem Muster bei einer Veranstaltung in Erfurt, DDR, am 20. Februar 1990.
Die zentrale Figur ist Helmut Kohl.

Un avenir démocratique. Des Allemands de
l'Est ont un premier avant-goût de campagne
électorale à Erfurt (Allemagne de l'Est), le
20 février 1990. Helmut Kohl est le personnage
central de la manifestation.

BARRY BATCHELOR/PA

The joys of devolution. Welsh supporters of devolution celebrate their
victory in the referendum, 19 September 1997. The 'yes' vote ensured that
a measure of self-government would return to Wales.

Das Glück der Regionalisierung. Walisische Anhänger der Dezentralisation
feiern ihren Sieg beim Referendum, 19. September 1997. Das „Ja" bei der
Abstimmung sicherte Wales ein gewisses Maß an Selbstverwaltung.

Les joies de la dévolution. Des partisans gallois de la dévolution célèbrent
leur victoire au referendum, le 19 septembre 1997. Les « oui » ont assuré le
retour de l'autodétermination au Pays de Galles.

DAVID CHESKIN/PA

The perils of independence. British Prime Minister Tony Blair gives of his dramatic best at the Royal Scottish Academy of Music and Drama, Glasgow, as he counsels against Scottish independence, 5 February 1999.

Die Gefahren der Unabhängigkeit. In der Royal Scottish Academy of Music and Drama von Glasgow wirft sich der britische Premierminister Tony Blair in dramatische Pose und plädiert gegen ein unabhängiges Schottland, 5. Februar 1999.

Les dangers de l'indépendance. Le Premier ministre britannique Tony Blair joue dans le registre dramatique à la Royal Scottish Academy of Music and Drama de Glasgow en déconseillant l'indépendance de l'Écosse, le 5 février 1999.

ALAN ABU HOSSAM/EPA/PA

Old homes, new ways... Palestinian members of the Isa Jibril family watch in dismay as Israeli bulldozers flatten their home in the Tekoa area of Bethlehem, 18 June 1998. In all, six houses were demolished.

Alte Heimat, neue Wege ... Entsetzt verfolgen palästinensische Mitglieder der Isa-Jibril-Familie, wie israelische Bulldozer ihre Häuser in Tekoa nahe Bethlehem niederwalzen, 18. Juni 1998. Insgesamt wurden sechs Häuser abgerissen.

Vieilles maisons, nouvelles voies ... Des membres de la famille palestinienne d'Isa Jibril assistent avec désespoir à la destruction de leur maison du quartier de Tekoa, près de Bethlehem, par les bulldozers israéliens, le 18 juin 1998. Six maisons furent démolies.

MANOOCHER DEGHATI/EPA/PA

Old ways, new homes… A Bedouin shepherd guides his flock past a new housing complex for Jewish settlers at Maale Adummim on the outskirts of Jerusalem, 12 August 1996.

Alte Wege, neue Heimat … Ein Beduinen-Schäfer führt seine Herde durch den neuen Wohnkomplex für jüdische Siedler in Maale Adummim, am Stadtrand von Jerusalem, 12. August 1996.

Anciennes voies, nouvelles maisons… Un berger bédouin dirige son troupeau devant le nouveau lotissement édifié pour les colons israéliens à Maale Adummim, dans la banlieue de Jérusalem, le 12 août 1996.

SEAN GALLUP/LIAISON AGENCY

A period of adjustment. Depositors and customers of the Czech bank
Ekoagrobanka gather in front of the Prague branch after predictions
that the bank was about to collapse, 11 January 1996.

Kursberichtigungen. Anleger und Kunden der tschechischen Bank
Ekoagrobanka sammeln sich nach Konkursgerüchten vor der Prager
Filiale, 11. Januar 1996.

Une période d'adaptation. Déposants et clients de la banque tchèque
Ekoagrobanka se rassemblent devant sa succursale pragoise après la
diffusion d'une rumeur de faillite de la banque, le 11 janvier 1996.

A fistful of euros. Peroza Ahmad of Thomas Cook displays travellers' cheques in the new euro currency, Dubai, United Arab Emirates, 10 January 1999. The launch of the euro was greeted with rather less enthusiasm in Europe.

Für eine Hand voll Euros … Peroza Ahmad von der Thomas-Cook-Filiale in Dubai, Vereinigte Arabische Emirate, präsentiert in Euro ausgestellte Travellerschecks, 10. Januar 1999. In Europa selbst wurde die Ankunft der neuen Währung mit weniger Enthusiasmus aufgenommen.

Les mains pleines d'euros. Peroza Ahmad, de l'agence Thomas Cook de Dubaï (Émirats arabes unis), montre des travellers' cheques émis dans la nouvelle devise européenne le 10 janvier 1999. Le lancement de l'euro fut salué avec un peu moins d'enthousiasme en Europe.

YANNIS BEHRAKIS/REUTERS/ARCHIVE PHOTOS

The curse of the pyramids. Free-market dealers trade in hard currency outside the Central Bank, Tirana, Albania, 31 January 1997. Following the collapse of pyramid investment schemes, Albanians rushed to buy 'hard' currency.

Der Fluch der Pyramiden. Freie Händler bieten vor der Zentralbank von Tirana, Albanien, harte Devisen zum Kauf an, 31. Januar 1997. Nach dem Zusammenbruch des „Pyramiden"-Investitionsfonds stürzten sich die Albaner auf „harte" Währungen.

La malédiction des pyramides. Des revendeurs sur le marché libre s'échangent des devises fortes devant la Central Bank de Tirana, en Albanie, le 31 janvier 1997. Les Albanais se précipitèrent pour acheter des devises « fortes » après l'effondrement des plans d'investissement pyramidaux.

On the same day, Albanians sell their blood at a Tirana hospital. The exchange rate was $24 for a pint.

Am selben Tag: In einem Krankenhaus in Tirana „verkaufen" Albaner ihr Blut zu einem Tageskurs von 24$ für etwas mehr als einen halben Liter.

Le même jour, d'autres Albanais vendent leur sang dans un hôpital de Tirana. Le taux de change était de 24 dollars pour un demi-litre.

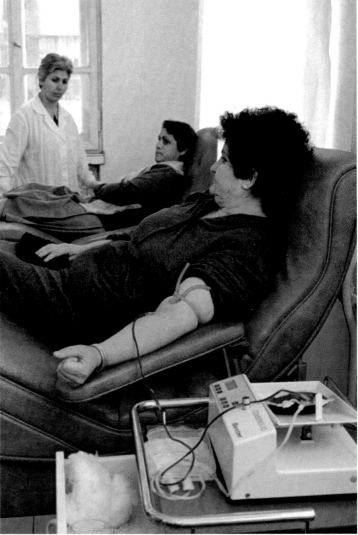

ARBEN CELI/REUTERS/ARCHIVE PHOTOS

MIKE FIALA/LIAISON AGENCY

British withdrawal. Members of the Black Watch march across the parade ground
at the Royal Navy headquarters in Hong Kong, 30 June 1997. It was the night when
Britain relinquished control of its former colony.

Britischer Rückzug. Mitglieder der Black Watch marschieren über den Exerzierplatz
des Royal-Navy-Hauptquartiers von Hongkong, 30. Juni 1997. An diesem Abend
gaben die Briten offiziell die Kontrolle über ihre ehemalige Kolonie zurück.

Retrait britannique. Des membres de la garde noire défilent sur le champ de parade
du quartier général de la Royal Navy à Hong-Kong, le 30 juin 1997. C'était la nuit
où les Anglais rendirent le contrôle de son ancienne colonie à la Chine.

STRINGER/REUTERS/ARCHIVE PHOTOS

Chinese advance. Troops of the Chinese People's
Liberation Army at a ceremony on the same day in
Shenzhen, shortly before leaving for Hong Kong.

Chinesischer Vormarsch. Truppen der chinesischen Volksbefreiungsarmee bei einer Zeremonie am selben Tag in
Shenzhen, kurz vor ihrem Aufbruch nach Hongkong.

L'avance chinoise. Les troupes de l'Armée de libération
du peuple chinois lors d'une cérémonie le même jour à
Shenzhen, peu avant leur départ pour Hong-Kong.

NIURKA BARROSA/EPA/PA

Happy to stay. A dance display by Cuban children to celebrate the
31st anniversary of the death of Che Guevara, Plaza de la Revolución,
Havana, 8 October 1998. The image on the wall is Che's.

Die einen sind froh zu bleiben … Mit einer Tanzvorführung feiern kubani-
sche Kinder den 31. Todestag Che Guevaras auf dem Platz der Revolution
in Havanna, 8. Oktober 1998. Das Wandbild zeigt den Revolutionär.

Heureux de rester. Un spectacle de danse par des enfants cubains pour la
célébration du 31ᵉ anniversaire de la mort de Che Guevara, Plaza de la
Revolución, à la Havane, le 8 octobre 1998. Le mur est décoré par une
représentation du Che.

EPA/PA

Desperate to leave. A woman supports her daughter as they prepare to climb aboard an improvised raft off the coast of Cuba, 23 September 1994. They were among thousands who sought a new life in the United States.

… die anderen können nicht warten zu fliehen. Eine Frau stützt ihre Tochter, bevor die beiden an Bord eines selbst gezimmerten Floßes von der kubanischen Küste aufbrechen, 23. September 1994. Zwei von Tausenden, die in den USA einen Neuanfang suchten.

Désespéré de vivre. Au large des côtes cubaines, une femme soutient sa fille avant de grimper à bord d'un radeau improvisé, le 23 septembre 1994. Ils faisaient partie de ces milliers de Cubains partis refaire une nouvelle vie aux États-Unis.

CHRISTOPHER MORRIS/BLACK STAR/COLORIFIC!

The age-old problems of cold and hunger return to the poor and elderly on Moscow's streets in the economic meltdown faced by the Russian state, 1999. Was this the best that the new order had to offer?

Der alte Kampf gegen Kälte und Hunger kehrt auf Moskaus Straßen zurück. Vor allem die Armen und Alten hatten unter der russischen Wirtschaftskrise von 1999 zu leiden. Waren das die Segnungen der „neuen Weltordnung"?

Les pauvres et les vieux Moscovites réapprennent le froid et la faim dans les rues de Moscou à la suite des bouleversements qu'a connus l'État russe en 1999. Était-ce le mieux que pouvait offrir le nouvel ordre économique ?

CHRISTOPHER MORRIS/BLACK STAR/COLORIFIC!

Communist hard-liners would almost certainly have labelled the protagonists in Moscow's exclusive Club Soho 'decadent hyenas'. Was lap dancing the best that the new order had to offer?

Kommunistische Hardliner hätten die Protagonisten des exklusiven Moskauer Nachtclubs Soho sicherlich als „dekadente Hyänen" bezeichnet. War Tabledancing das Beste, was die „neue Weltordnung" zu bieten hatte?

Les communistes purs et durs auraient certainement qualifié de « hyènes décadentes » ces clients du très exclusif Club Soho de Moscou. Ce genre de spectacle était-il le mieux que pouvait offrir le nouvel ordre économique ?

4. Pre-millennium tension
Jahrtausend-Fieber
Tensions d'avant-millénaire

Two-month-old Namu Otani undergoes a radiation check at
Tokaimura Civil Center, 8 October 1999. Two days earlier, Japan
had suffered the worst nuclear accident since Chernobyl, at the
JCO Nuclear Fuel Plant.

Der zwei Monate alte Namu Otani bei einer Ultraschallunter-
suchung im Bürgerzentrum von Tokaimura, 8. Oktober 1999.
Zwei Tage zuvor ereignete sich in der japanischen JCO Nuclear
Fuel Plant die schlimmste Atomkatastrophe seit Tschernobyl.

Namu Otani, âgé de deux mois, subit un contrôle de radiation au
Tokaimura Civil Center, le 8 octobre 1999. Deux jours plus tôt,
le Japon avait subi le pire accident nucléaire depuis Tchernobyl,
survenu au JCO Nuclear Fuel Plant.

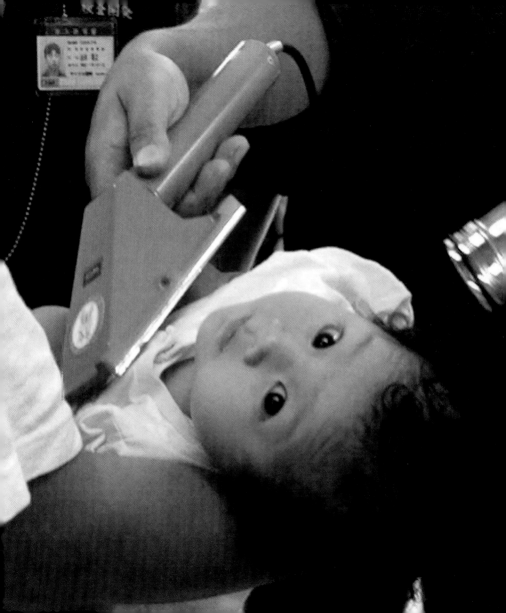

4. Pre-millennium tension
Jahrtausend-Fieber
Tensions d'avant-millénaire

For much of the decade, the oncoming Millennium concentrated the minds of reformers and radicals, politicians and protesters. Every cause and every campaign seemed to be under sentence of execution – so much to be done before the year 2000, and so little time to do it. Schemers and counter-schemers locked minds over the future of the planet. There were battles over the causes and effects of pollution, over the pros and cons of genetically modified food, over the future of humanity.

Those with extreme views suggested, as the 1990s tottered towards the Millennium, that the world would soon end. There were massacres in schools at the Scottish town of Dunblane, and at Littleton, Colorado; on the subway in Tokyo; and at a tourist resort in Port Arthur. There were floods in Bangladesh and Europe, earthquakes in California and Japan. Zealots sold all they had and hurried to selected vantage points from which they could ascend en masse to heaven. In scenes reminiscent of the debauched last days of Ancient Rome, people sniffed and snorted their preferred drugs, threw caution and morality to the wild winds, ate, drank and were merry. The planet, racked by storms that could have been the result of global warming, somehow held together.

Politiker, Demonstranten, Reformer und Radikale brachten einige Zeit des Jahrzehnts mit Gedanken über das herannahende Millennium zu. Jede Angelegenheit oder Kampagne hatte schnell umgesetzt zu werden – so viel musste vor dem Jahr 2000 noch erledigt werden, und so wenig Zeit blieb dafür. Planer und Gegenplaner beschäftigten sich intensiv mit der Zukunft des Planeten. So gab es Auseinandersetzungen über Ursache und Wirkung der Umweltverschmutzung, über das Für und Wider gentechnisch veränderter Lebensmittel, über die Zukunft der Menschheit.

Während die neunziger Jahre in Richtung Millennium torkelten, beschworen Vertreter extremer Ansichten das bevorstehende Weltende. Es gab die Massaker an den Schulen der schottischen Stadt Dunblane und in Littleton, Colorado, in der U-Bahn von Tokio und in einem Touristencamp in Port Arthur. Flutkatastrophen erschütterten Bangladesch und Europa, Erdbeben wüteten in Kalifornien und Japan. Religiöse Fanatiker verkauften all ihre Habe und versammelten sich an bestimmten Orten, von denen aus sie in Massen zum Himmel aufzusteigen glaubten. In einem Szenario, das an die ausschweifenden letzten Tage des Alten Roms erinnerte, schnupften die Menschen ihre Lieblingsdrogen, schlugen Vorsicht und Moral in den Wind, aßen, tranken und feierten. Der Planet wurde von Stürmen erschüttert – die durchaus auf die globale Erwärmung zurückzuführen sein könnten –, blieb aber letztendlich doch heil.

L'approche du millénaire a focalisé pendant une grande partie de la décennie la pensée des réformateurs, des radicaux, des politiques et des manifestants. Toutes les causes et toutes les campagnes semblaient devoir s'exécuter immédiatement – tant à faire avant l'an 2000, et si peu de temps pour le réaliser. Prévisionnistes et anti-prévisionnistes bloquaient les esprits sur l'avenir de la planète. Il y eut des discussions sur les causes et les effets de la pollution, sur les preuves de la réalité d'un réchauffement global de la planète et sur l'avenir de l'humanité.

Plus l'on s'approchait du millénaire, plus il y avait de visionnaires extrêmes annonçant l'imminence de la fin du monde. Il y eut des massacres dans les écoles de Dunblane en Écosse et de Littleton au Colorado, dans le métro de Tokyo, et dans une station touristique de Port Arthur. Il y eut des inondations au Bangladesh et en Europe, des tremblements de terre en Californie et au Japon. Des fanatiques vendirent tout ce qu'ils possédaient avant de se rassembler en masse dans des lieux d'où ils pensaient accéder au paradis. Dans des scènes dignes des derniers jours de décadence de la Rome antique, des gens reniflaient ou prisaient leurs drogues favorites, jetant aux orties toute prudence et morale, mangeant, buvant et s'amusant. Battue par des tempêtes qui auraient pu résulter de son réchauffement global, la planète continuait de tenir bon quand même.

(Opposite)
Fumigating against
malaria, El Salvador,
29 September 1999.
(Right) After the
deluge: a flooded
cemetery in
Trujillo, Peru,
12 February 1998.

(Gegenüberliegende
Seite) Ausräuche-
rung der Malaria
in El Salvador,
29. September 1999.
(Rechts) Nach der
Flutkatastrophe:
ein überschwemmter
Friedhof in
Trujillo, Peru,
12. Februar 1998.

(Ci-contre) Fumiga-
tions contre la mala-
ria au Salvador, le
29 septembre 1999.
(À droite) Après
le déluge dans un
cimetière de Trujillo,
au Pérou,
le 12 février 1998.

SILVIA IZQUIERDO/REUTERS/ARCHIVE PHOTOS

EPA/PA

(Above) The oil tanker *Erika* breaks up off the coast of Brittany, France, 13 December 1999. (Opposite) Not long after, an oil-soaked grebe is rescued from the beaches of Noirmoutier. Tens of thousands of sea-birds died.

(Oben) Der Öltanker *Erika* bricht vor der bretonischen Küste, Frankreich, auseinander, 13. Dezember 1999. (Gegenüberliegende Seite) Nur wenig später wird dieser ölverschmierte Seetaucher am Strand von Noirmoutier aufgegriffen. Zehntausende von Meeresvögeln fielen der Havarie zum Opfer.

(Ci-dessus) Le pétrolier *Erika* se brise au large des côtes bretonnes, le 13 décembre 1999. (Ci-contre) Peu de temps après, une grèbe mazoutée est recueillie sur les plages de Noirmoutier. Des dizaines de milliers d'oiseaux périrent.

GREENPEACE/ARCHIVE PHOTOS

A new battleground. A field of corn near Freiburg, southern Germany, after Greenpeace activists had attached a warning label. The 400-metre square banner reads: 'Attention – genetically modified – X.'

Ein neues Schlachtfeld. Greenpeace-Aktivisten haben auf diesem Kornfeld nahe Freiburg ein 400 Quadratmeter großes Banner ausgerollt, um vor den Gefahren der Gentechnologie zu warnen.

Un nouveau champ de bataille. Des activistes de Greenpeace ont apposé un panneau de 400 m² dans un champ de blé près de Fribourg (sud de l'Allemagne), où il est écrit : « Attention ! Génétiquement modifié – X ».

Greenpeace raiders destroy a GM experimental crop in Lyng, England, 26 July 1999. Thirty of them were arrested, including local farmer and Greenpeace Executive Director Peter Melchett. At their subsequent trial all were acquitted.

Greenpeace-Aktivisten zerstören ein Versuchsfeld mit genmanipulierten Pflanzen, Lyng, England, 26. Juli 1999. Insgesamt wurden 30 Personen verhaftet, darunter ein ortsansässiger Bauer und der Greenpeace-Geschäftsführer Peter Melchett. In der folgenden Gerichtsverhandlung wurden jedoch alle freigesprochen.

Des commandos de Greenpeace détruisent un champ expérimental de plantes génétiquement modifiées à Lyng (Angleterre), le 26 juillet 1999. Trente d'entre eux furent arrêtés, dont un paysan de la région et le directeur général de Greenpeace, Peter Melchett. Ils furent tous acquittés lors du procès.

EPA/PA

Demonstrators bring the streets of Seattle to a standstill as they protest at the
World Trade Organisation Summit, 2 December 1999. This section of the
protest was directed against Bovine Growth Hormones (BGH).

Beim Gipfeltreffen der Welthandelsorganisation (WTO) blockierten
Demonstranten die Straßen von Seattle, 2. Dezember 1999. Diese Protest-
aktion richtete sich gegen Wachstumshormone in der Rinderzucht. „No BGH
in this body" bedeutet „Kein Wachstumshormon in diesem Körper".

Des manifestants – qui s'opposent ici aux hormones de croissance pour
les bovins – défilent dans les rues de Seattle à l'occasion du sommet de
l'Organisation du Commerce Mondial, le 2 décembre 1999.

ANTHONY BOLANTE/REUTERS/ARCHIVE PHOTOS

Robocops – in reality members of the Seattle Police Department – prepare to defend the World Trade Organisation headquarters, 29 November 1999. They underestimated the number of officers needed, and the following day a curfew was imposed.

Diese „Robocops" – in Wirklichkeit Mitglieder des Seattle Police Department – bereiten sich auf die Verteidigung des Hauptquartiers der Welthandelsorganisation vor, 29. November 1999. Die Zahl der benötigten Polizeikräfte wurde weit unterschätzt, am nächsten Tag verhängte man eine Ausgangssperre.

Les Robocops – c'est-à-dire les sections spéciales de la police de Seattle – se préparent à défendre le quartier général de l'Organisation du Commerce Mondial, le 29 novembre 1999. Ayant sous-estimé le nombre de policiers nécessaires, il fallut imposer un couvre-feu le lendemain.

ZAHID HUSSEIN/REUTERS/ARCHIVE PHOTOS

(Opposite and above) Two perspectives on the Bomb. (Above) Pakistani youths with a model
of a Ghauri missile in a night rally, Karachi, 31 May 1998. Some saw the possession of nuclear capability
as a benefit to their country.

(Oben und gegenüberliegende Seite) Zwei Sichtweisen auf die Bombe. (Oben) Pakistanische Jugendliche
feiern bei einem nächtlichen Straßenkorso in Karatschi mit einer Nachbildung der Ghauri-Rakete,
31. Mai 1998. Viele betrachteten den Besitz von Nuklearwaffen als Vorteil für ihr Land.

(Ci-contre et ci-dessus) Deux opinions sur la Bombe. (Ci-dessus) De jeunes Pakistanais défilent
avec une maquette d'un missile Ghauri lors d'une manifestation nocturne à Karachi, le 31 mai 1998.
Certains considéraient comme un bien pour leur pays la possession de moyens nucléaires.

KAMAL KISHORE/REUTERS/ARCHIVE PHOTOS

Anti-bomb protesters gather in New Delhi, India, 16 May 1998 (above). The march was held following a series of underground nuclear tests by the Indian Government in the northern state of Rajasthan.

Gegner der Atombombe bei einer Versammlung in Neu-Delhi, Indien, 16. Mai 1998 (oben). Die Kundgebung war die Reaktion auf eine Serie von unterirdischen Raketentests der indischen Regierung in der nördlichen Provinz Rajasthan.

Des manifestants antinucléaires se sont rassemblés à New Delhi, en Inde, le 16 mai 1998 (ci-dessus). Cette marche de protestation fut organisée à la suite des essais nucléaires souterrains réalisés par le gouvernement indien dans l'état du Rajasthan, au nord du pays.

An anti-abortion poster is paraded outside the US Supreme Court, Washington, DC, 1996. It was the 23rd anniversary of legal abortions.

Anlässlich des 23. Jahrestages der Legalisierung von Abtreibungen wird vor dem US Supreme Court in Washington, D.C., ein Anti-Abtreibungs-Plakat mit der Aufschrift „Schande" aufgestellt, 1996.

Une affiche contre l'avortement est brandie devant le siège de la Cour suprême des États-Unis, à Washington DC, en 1996, lors du 23ᵉ anniversaire de la légalisation de l'avortement.

WIN McNAMEE/REUTERS/ARCHIVE PHOTOS

Parodying a multinational corporation: a workman completes a giant billboard advertising the link between smoking and impotence, Hollywood, 23 April 1999.

Parodie auf einen weltweit operierenden Großkonzern: Ein Arbeiter legt letzte Hand an eine überdimensionale Werbetafel, die auf den Zusammenhang zwischen dem Rauchen und Impotenz hinweist. Hollywood, 23. April 1999.

À Hollywood, un ouvrier achève le montage d'un panneau géant, parodie de la publicité d'une multinationale, soulignant la relation de cause à effet entre le tabagisme et l'impuissance, le 23 avril 1999.

ROSE PROUSER/REUTERS/ARCHIVE PHOTOS

DAVID BUTOW/BLACK STAR/COLORIFIC!

Riots in Los Angeles, April/May 1992. Fifty-eight people were killed, 2,200 were injured and damage was estimated at over $1 billion. The rioting broke out soon after the acquittal of the four police officers on trial for the beating of Rodney King.

Aufstände in Los Angeles, April/Mai 1992. 85 Menschen wurden getötet, 2200 verletzt, der Sachschaden betrug über eine Milliarde US-Dollar. Die Unruhen brachen kurz nach dem Freispruch für die vier Polizisten aus, die Rodney King brutal zusammengeschlagen hatten.

Émeutes à Los Angeles, avril-mai 1992. Cinquante-huit personnes furent tuées et 2200 blessées, avec des dégâts estimés à plus d'un milliard de dollars. Les émeutes se déclenchèrent peu après l'acquittement des quatre policiers jugés pour avoir battu Rodney King.

Rodney King shows some of the scars that resulted from the beating of 3 March 1991. The incident was recorded by a passer-by on his video camera.

Rodney King zeigt einige der Narben, die ihm am 3. März 1991 von der Polizei zugefügt wurden. Ein Passant hatte das Ereignis mit seiner Videokamera aufgenommen.

Rodney King montre les traces des coups que lui ont donnés les policiers, le 3 mars 1991. L'incident avait été enregistré au caméscope par un passant.

ROGER SANDLER/COLORIFIC!

SAM MIRCOVICH/REUTERS/ARCHIVE PHOTOS

On the freeway. The jeep carrying O J Simpson is pursued by a posse of police cars along the Los Angeles Thru'way, California, 17 June 1994. The chase was just one bizarre episode in many that followed a double murder.

Auf dem Freeway. O. J. Simpsons Jeep wird von einem ganzen Aufgebot an Polizeiwagen quer durch Los Angeles verfolgt, Kalifornien, 17. Juni 1994. Diese Jagd war nur eine von vielen absonderlichen Episoden, die sich im Fall eines Doppelmordes noch abspielen sollten.

Sur l'autoroute. La jeep transportant O. J. Simpson est poursuivie par une meute de voitures de police sur la Los Angeles Thru'way, en Californie, le 17 juin 1994. Cette chasse à l'homme fut un des nombreux épisodes étranges qui suivirent le double meurtre.

VINCE BUCCI/REUTERS/ARCHIVE PHOTOS

On the stand. O J Simpson raises his hands to the jury at his trial, 21 June 1995. The prosecution were seeking to show that Simpson's hands could fit into gloves found at the scene of the murder.

Im Gerichtssaal. Während seines Prozesses hebt O. J. Simpson die Hände in Richtung der Geschworenen, 21. Juni 1995. Die Anklage wollte beweisen, dass Simpson die Handschuhe passten, die am Tatort gefunden wurden.

À la barre. O. J. Simpson lève les mains vers le jury lors de son procès, le 21 juin 1995. L'accusation tentait d'établir que les gants trouvés sur le lieu du crime pouvaient correspondre aux mains de Simpson.

Participants in the Million Youth March, Harlem, New York, 5 September 1998 (opposite), and stewards at the Million Man March in Washington, DC (above), 16 October 1995. Both marches were intended to bring attention to continued racial discrimination in the US.

(Gegenüberliegende Seite) Teilnehmer am Million Youth March (Marsch der Millionen Jugendlichen), Harlem, New York, 5. September 1998. (Oben) Ordner beim Million Man March in Washington, D.C., 16. Oktober 1995. Beide Veranstaltungen wollten Aufmerksamkeit für die fortwährende Rassen-diskriminierung in den USA schaffen.

Des participants à la Million Youth March de New York, le 5 septembre 1998 (ci-contre), et des stewards à la Million Man March de Washington DC (ci-dessus), le 16 octobre 1995. Ces deux manifestations avaient pour but d'attirer l'attention sur la pérennité de la discrimination raciale aux États-Unis.

LAURA I. CAMDEN/LIAISON AGENCY

Right-wing bigots warm their memories
under the Ku Klux Klan's fiery cross, Hico,
near Austin, Texas, May 1994. Their
numbers were dwindling.

Rechtsextreme Fanatiker wärmen ihre
Erinnerung unter dem brennenden Kreuz,
Symbol des Ku-Klux-Klans, Hico, nahe
Austin, Texas, Mai 1994. Die Zahl der
Anhänger dieser Bewegung allerdings sank.

Des fanatiques de droite réchauffent leurs
souvenirs autour de la croix de feu du
Ku Klux Klan, à Hico, près d'Austin (Texas),
en mai 1994. Leur nombre était toutefois en
diminution.

CHRISTIAN IRRGANG/FOCUS/COLORIFIC!

The right-wing politician Jörg Haider campaigns during the 1995 Austrian elections. Haider later resigned as leader of the far-right Freedom Party, but held the post of Governor of Carpinthia province in southern Austria.

Der rechtsradikale Politiker Jörg Haider bei einer Veranstaltung im Wahlkampf 1995. Später trat Haider als Vorsitzender der rechtsextremen Freiheitlichen Partei Österreichs (FPÖ) zurück, blieb aber Landeshauptmann von Kärnten in Südösterreich.

L'ultra-droitiste Jörg Haider fait sa campagne électorale pour les élections autrichiennes de 1995. Haider démissionna ensuite de son poste de chef du Freiheitliche Partei, un parti d'extrême-droite, mais conserva le poste de gouverneur de la province de Carinthie (sud de l'Autriche).

SIEGBERT HEILAND/EPA/PA

Neo-Nazis of the German People's Union parade through the streets of Halle in former East Germany, November 1995. In the Saxony-Anhalt state elections that followed they won 12.9 per cent of the vote.

Neonazistische Anhänger der Deutschen Volksunion (DVU) marschieren durch die Straßen von Halle in der ehemaligen DDR, November 1995. Bei den folgenden Landtagswahlen in Sachsen-Anhalt holte die DVU 12,9 Prozent der Stimmen.

Des néonazis de l'Union du peuple allemand paradent dans les rues de Halle, une ville de l'ancienne Allemagne de l'Est, en novembre 1995. Ils remportèrent 12,9% des voix aux élections du Land de Saxe qui suivirent.

FRANCES M ROBERTS/LIAISON AGENCY

Like minds, like bodies. In the absence of legally recognised marriages, gay and lesbian couples hold 'commitment' ceremonies in Bryant Park, 16 June 1996. For an alternative American view, see opposite.

Gleich und Gleich gesellt sich gern. In Ermangelung einer legalen Grundlage für gleichgeschlechtliche Ehen, halten schwule und lesbische Paare im Bryant Park eigene „Hochzeitszeremonien" ab, 16. Juni 1996. Eine amerikanische Gegenmeinung vertritt der Herr auf der gegenüberliegenden Seite.

Corps et âmes. En l'absence de mariage légalement reconnu, des couples homosexuels organisent des cérémonies d'« engagement » au Bryant Park, le 16 juin 1996. Voir ci-contre l'opinion américaine adverse.

Split opinion.
The Reverend Fred
Phelps of the
Westboro Baptist
Church, Topeka,
Kansas, flaunts his
'God hates fags' sign,
22 November 1998.

Geteilter Meinung.
Reverend Fred
Phelps von der
Baptistengemeinde
Westboro in Topeka,
Kansas, reckt ein
Schild mit der
Aufschrift „Gott
hasst Homos"
in die Höhe,
22. November 1998.

Une opinion divisée.
Le révérend Fred
Phelps, de la
Westboro Baptist
Church de Topeka
(Kansas), brandit sa
banderole « Dieu
hait les pédés », le
22 novembre 1998.

TIM BOYLE/LIAISON AGENCY

REUTERS/ARCHIVE PHOTOS

SHELLY KATZ/LIAISON AGENCY

Prophets and losses 1. (Above) David Koresh, leader of the Branch Davidian cult. In April 1993 he and his followers died during an FBI raid on the cult's headquarters at Waco, Texas (above right).

(Oben) David Koresh, Führer der Davidianer-Sekte. Im April 1993 fiel Koresh mit seinen Jüngern einem FBI-Angriff auf das Hauptquartier der Sekte in Waco, Texas, zum Opfer (oben rechts).

(Ci-dessus) David Koresh, chef de la secte de la Branche Davidienne. En avril 1993, ses fidèles et lui-même furent tués lors d'un raid du FBI sur le quartier général de la secte à Waco, Texas (en haut à droite).

EPA/PA

EPA/PA

Prophets and losses 2. (Above) Shoko Asahara, guru of Aum Supreme Truth, October 1990. In March 1995 Asahara released nerve gas in the Tokyo subway, asphyxiating thousands of people (above right).

(Oben) Shoko Asahara, Guru von Aum Supreme Truth, Oktober 1990. Im März 1995 setzte Asahara in der Tokioter U-Bahn Nervengas frei – Tausende von Menschen erstickten (oben rechts).

(Ci-dessus) Shoko Asahara, gourou d'Aum Supreme Truth, en octobre 1990. En mars 1995, Asahara commettait un attentat au gaz sarin dans le métro de Tokyo, asphyxiant des milliers de gens (en haut à droite).

On 19 April 1995 a truck carrying 2,000 kilos of explosives destroyed the Federal Bureau of Alcohol, Tobacco and Firearms, Oklahoma City.

Am 19. April 1995 zerstörte ein mit 2000 Kilo Sprengstoff beladener LKW das amerikanische Bundesamt für Alkohol, Tabak und Feuerwaffen in Oklahoma City.

Le 19 avril 1995, un camion transportant deux tonnes d'explosifs détruisait le Federal Bureau of Alcohol, Tobacco and Firearms de Oklahoma City.

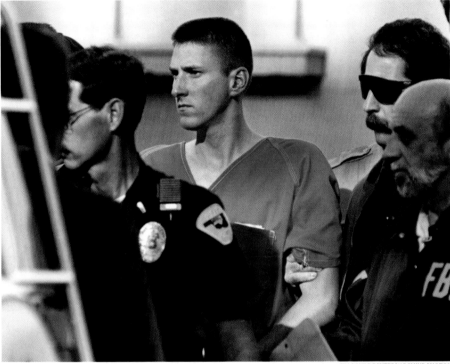

JIM BOURG/REUTERS/ARCHIVE PHOTOS

Police later arrested Timothy McVeigh for the offence. (Above) Two days after the bombing McVeigh (centre) leaves the Noble County Courthouse, accompanied by FBI agents.

Wenig später wurde Timothy McVeigh als Täter verhaftet. (Oben) Zwei Tage nach dem Bombenanschlag verlässt McVeigh (Bildmitte) in Begleitung von FBI-Agenten das Gerichtsgebäude von Noble County.

La police arrêta Timothy McVeigh pour ce crime. (Ci-dessus) Deux jours après l'attentat à la bombe, McVeigh (au centre) quitte le palais de justice de Noble County, accompagné par des agents du FBI.

MARK LEFFINGEWELL/LIAISON AGENCY

Students at Columbine High School, Littleton, Colorado, rush for cover as shots are heard from inside their school building, 20 April 1999. Two former students, Eric Harris and Dylan Klebold, were responsible.

Schüler der Columbine High School von Littleton, Colorado, eilen in Deckung, als im Inneren des Gebäudes Schüsse fallen, 20. April 1999. Zwei ehemalige Schüler, Eric Harris und Dylan Klebold, waren verantwortlich für die Tat.

Des étudiants de la Columbine High School de Littleton (Colorado) se précipitent à couvert en entendant des coups de feu tirés à l'intérieur de leur établissement, le 20 avril 1999, par deux anciens élèves, Eric Harris et Dylan Klebold.

MARK LEFFINGEWELL/LIAISON AGENCY

Other students watch from safety during the evacuation of the school. If the police were baffled as to what motive the youths could have had, the world was baffled by the suggestion that other students had advance knowledge of the intended massacre.

Als die Schule evakuiert wird, beobachten andere Schüler das Geschehen aus sicherer Distanz. Während die Polizei noch rätselte, welche Motive die Jugendlichen gehabt haben könnten, staunte die Welt, dass einige Schüler offenbar schon vorher von dem geplanten Massaker gewusst hatten.

D'autres élèves assistent à l'évacuation de leur école depuis leur abri. Si la police fut déconcertée par les motifs des deux jeunes gens, le monde fut dérouté par l'idée que d'autres étudiants connaissaient à l'avance le massacre prévu.

ARCHIVE PHOTOS

(Left) Lipstick on your collar... Monica Lewinsky embraces Bill Clinton outside the White House, 11 June 1996. (Above) ...and stains on your dress. Lewinsky's blue dress, presented as evidence by Kenneth Starr.

(Links) Lippenstift am Kragen ... Monica Lewinsky umarmt Bill Clinton vor dem Weißen Haus, 11. Juni 1996. (Oben) ... und Flecken auf dem blauen Kleid. Es wurde von Kenneth Starr als Beweisstück präsentiert.

(À gauche) Du rouge à lèvres sur ton col... Monica Lewinsky embrasse Bill Clinton devant la Maison Blanche, le 11 juin 1996. (Ci-dessus) ... et des taches sur ta robe. La robe bleue de Monica, présentée à titre de preuve par Kenneth Starr.

Stating the Presidential position... Bill Clinton (opposite) denies having sexual relationships with 'that woman', Monica Lewinsky (right).

Standpunkt und Stellung des Präsidenten ... Bill Clinton (gegen-überliegende Seite) streitet eine sexuelle Beziehung zu „dieser Frau" – Monica Lewinsky (rechts) – ab.

Marquer la position présidentielle ... Bill Clinton (ci-contre) nie avoir eu des relations sexuelles avec « cette femme », Monica Lewinsky (à droite).

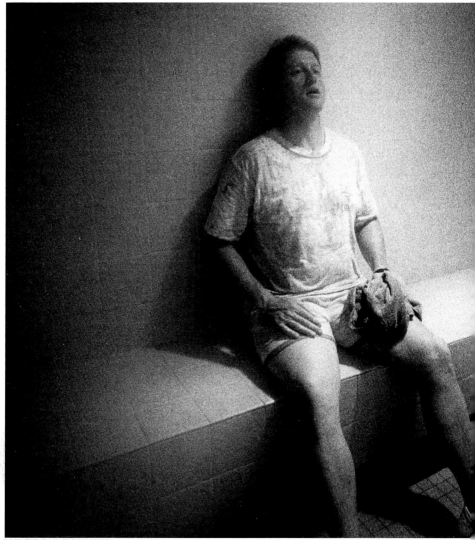

Bill Clinton sweats it out in the sauna of a
New York City hotel during his campaign
seeking nomination as the Democratic
candidate, 1992.

In der Sauna eines New Yorker Hotels kommt
Bill Clinton ins Schwitzen. Die Aufnahme
entstand zur Zeit seines Nominierungswahl-
kampfes zum Präsidentschaftskandidaten der
Demokraten, 1992.

Bill Clinton transpire dans le sauna d'un
hôtel de New York lors de la campagne pour
sa nomination comme candidat démocrate
en 1992.

5. Entertainment
Unterhaltung
Les divertissements

Jerry Seinfeld, stand-up comedian and star of the hugely successful TV sitcom *Seinfeld*. He claimed the show was 'about nothing', but over five series it was brilliantly crafted and superbly performed.

Jerry Seinfeld, Komiker und Hauptdarsteller der außerordentlich erfolgreichen Fernsehsitcom *Seinfeld*. Obwohl er stets behauptete, in der Show ginge es „um rein gar nichts", brachte es Seinfeld auf fünf brillant konzipierte und exzellent gespielte Staffeln.

Jerry Seinfeld, comédien comique et vedette de *Seinfeld,* une série télé à succès. Ce show, qu'il annonçait comme étant « à propos de rien », se révéla en plus de cinq séries brillamment réalisé et magnifiquement animé.

5. Entertainment
Unterhaltung
Les divertissements

The cinema industry reached the end of the century on an upbeat note. Audiences were steadily growing, more films were being made, and Hollywood was regaining much of its glamour as well as its powers to shock. Magazines delightedly exposed the scandals that attached to the famous.

Seldom had the world-wide movie industry produced such a variety of films. Budgets soared for spectacular blockbusters, but there was a healthy market for the more modest, independently produced film. If computer animation lacked the subtlety and beauty of the best of old Walt Disney, its humour and vitality brought box office success.

At home, more people had more TVs, digital, cable or otherwise, and a plethora of channels from which to select. Such choice often meant that talent was spread a little more thinly, but every country had its popular home-grown soaps, and there were always repeats to fall back on. Now and then comedy was king, with a clutch of brilliant sitcoms from the United States, notably *Frasier, Seinfeld, Roseanne* and *The Larry Sanders Show,* and a healthy market for stand-up comedians.

There was still no business like show business.

Das Ende des Jahrhunderts sah die Filmindustrie im Aufschwung. Das Publikum wuchs stetig an, mehr Filme wurden produziert und Hollywood gewann einiges von seinem Glamour und der Fähigkeit zu schockieren zurück. In den Magazinen wurden die Skandale rund um die Stars dankbar aufgenommen.

Selten brachte die Filmindustrie eine solche Vielfalt auf die Leinwand. Während Schwindel erregende Budgets spektakuläre Publikumserfolge hervorbrachten, gab es auch einen Markt für bescheidenere, unabhängig produzierte Filme. Auch wenn Computeranimationen in puncto Schönheit und Feingefühl nicht an die besten Filme des alten Walt Disney heran-reichten – ihr Sinn für Humor und ihre Lebendigkeit sorgten doch für Kassenschlager.

In den eigenen vier Wänden verfügten mehr Menschen über mehr Fernsehgeräte, mit digitalem, Kabel- oder sonstigem Zugang und einer Unzahl von empfangbaren Kanälen. Die schiere Auswahl sorgte zwar nicht unbedingt für ein Mehr an Qualität und Talent; dennoch hatte jedes Land seine eigenen populären Seifenopern und genügend Wieder-holungen, auf die man zurückgreifen konnte. Zeitweise war die „Comedy" Königin der Genres mit brillanten Sitcoms aus den USA, etwa *Frasier, Seinfeld, Roseanne* und *The Larry Sanders Show* sowie einem florierenden Markt für Alleinunterhalter und Komiker.

Und immer noch galt: „There's no business like show business".

L'industrie cinématographique atteignait la fin du siècle sur une note optimiste. Le nombre des spectateurs augmentait régulièrement, de plus en plus de films étaient réalisés et Hollywood retrouvait une grande partie de son prestige et de son pouvoir de choquer. Les magazines exposaient délibérément les scandales frappant les célébrités.

L'industrie cinématographique mondiale avait rarement produit une telle diversité de films. Alors que les budgets augmentaient démesurément pour des films spectaculaires et à grand succès, il subsistait un marché bien portant pour les films plus modestes des pro-ductions indépendantes. Si les animations par ordinateur manquaient de la subtilité et de la beauté des meilleurs dessins animés de Walt Disney, elles les compensaient par leur humour et leur vitalité pour obtenir de bons chiffres au box office.

De plus en plus de gens disposent de plusieurs télévisions – numérique, câblée ou autre – leur offrant le choix entre une pléthore de chaînes, ce qui implique souvent une dispersion croissante des talents et de la qualité. Mais chaque pays a ses propres séries populaires et il est toujours possible de tomber sur une rediffusion. La comédie est toujours reine et se distingue par un éventail de sitcoms brillants venus des États-Unis, notamment *Frasier, Seinfeld, Roseanne* et *The Larry Sanders Show,* offrant de nombreuses scènes aux comiques.

Il n'y a toujours pas de business sans show business.

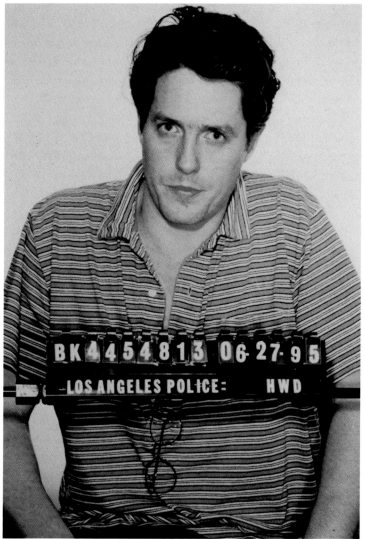

Two bookings and a scandal. Hugh Grant poses for the Los Angeles Police Department, 27 June 1995.

Zwei Festnahmen und ein Skandal. Hugh Grant posiert für das Los Angeles Police Department, 27. Juni 1995.

Deux complices et un scandale. Hugh Grant pose pour le Los Angeles Police Department, le 27 juin 1995.

LAPD/EPA/PA

Grant and Divine Brown (right) were arrested following a *tête à groin* incident in a car on Hollywood's Sunset Boulevard.

Grant und Divine Brown (rechts) wurden aufgrund ihres „Zusammen-stoßes" auf dem Rücksitz eines Wagens am Sunset Boulevard, Holly-wood, verhaftet.

Grant et Divine Brown (à droite) furent arrêtés en fâcheuse posture dans une voiture garée sur Sunset Boulevard à Hollywood.

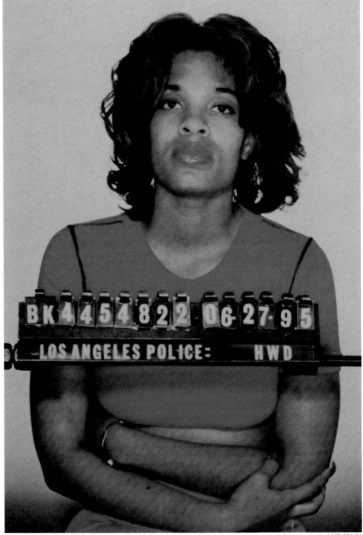

LAPD/EPA/PA

Gwyneth Paltrow, in a Ralph Lauren dress, sobs as she receives the Oscar for Best Actress for her role in *Shakespeare in Love*, 22 March 1999.

Gwyneth Paltrow – in einem Kleid von Ralph Lauren – nimmt schluchzend ihren Oscar für die beste Schauspielerin entgegen. Sie erhielt die Auszeichnung für ihre Rolle in *Shakespeare in Love*, 22. März 1999.

Gwyneth Paltrow, dans une robe de Ralph Lauren, fond en larmes en recevant l'Oscar de la meilleure actrice pour son rôle dans *Shakespeare in Love*, le 22 mars 1999.

EPA/PA

Ian McKellen and Emily Watson at the BAFTA Los Angeles tea party, Santa Monica, 21 March 1999, on the eve of the Oscar ceremonies. Both had been nominated – McKellen for *Gods and Monsters*, Watson for *Hilary and Jackie*.

Ian McKellen und Emily Watson bei einem Empfang der BAFTA (Britische Akademie für Film- und Fernsehkünste) in Santa Monica, Los Angeles, am 21. März 1999, dem Vorabend der Oscar-Verleihung. Beide waren nominiert – McKellen für *Gods and Monsters*, Watson für *Hilary and Jackie*.

Ian McKellen et Emily Watson lors d'un thé au BAFTA de Los Angeles, à Santa Monica, le 21 mars 1999, le soir de la cérémonie des Oscars. Tous deux avaient été sélectionnés : McKellen pour *Gods and Monsters*, et Watson pour *Hilary and Jackie*.

La Dolce Vita lives again. Italian film star Marcello Mastroianni (left) admires an admirer.

La Dolce Vita lebt wieder auf: Der italienische Filmstar Marcello Mastroianni (links) bewundert einen weiblichen Bewunderer.

La Dolce Vita revit. La vedette du cinéma italien Marcello Mastroianni (à gauche) admire une admiratrice.

The Godfather LXXIV. American film star Winona Ryder with her godfather, Timothy Leary. Ryder's father, Michael Horowitz, was Leary's archivist and with him co-authored an encyclopaedia of drugs.

The Godfather LXXIV. Die amerikanische Filmschauspielerin Winona Ryder mit ihrem Patenonkel Timothy Leary. Ryders leiblicher Vater, Michael Horowitz, war Learys Archivar und verfasste gemeinsam mit ihm eine Enzyklopädie über Drogen.

Le Parrain LXXIV. La vedette de cinéma américaine Winona Ryder avec son parrain, Timothy Leary. Le père de Winona, Michael Horowitz, était l'archiviste de Leary et son coauteur pour une encyclopédie des drogues.

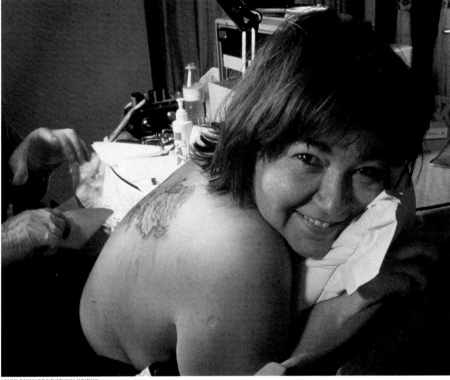

MARK RICHARDS/DOT/COLORIFIC!

In an unusually happy mood, Roseanne Barr relaxes at the tattooist's. Despite much off-screen tension and frequent rows between star and writers, the TV sitcom *Roseanne* was one of the biggest hits of the 1990s.

Eine ungewöhnlich gut gelaunte Roseanne Barr entspannt sich beim Tätowierer. Trotz großer Spannungen hinter der Kamera und häufiger Streitigkeiten zwischen Schauspielern und Autoren war die Fernsehsitcom *Roseanne* eine der erfolgreichsten der neunziger Jahre.

Exceptionnellement de bonne humeur, Roseanne Barr se détend chez le tatoueur. Malgré les nombreuses tensions hors écran et les fréquentes disputes entre la vedette et les scénaristes, le sitcom télé *Roseanne* fit l'une des meilleures audiences des années 1990.

The show they hate to love. Chat show host Jerry Springer (left) with two highly excitable friends.

Die Show, die man hasste und liebte. Talk-Showmaster Jerry Springer (links) mit zwei äußerst erregbaren Freundinnen.

Le show qu'ils détestent aimer. Un talk show accueille Jerry Springer (à gauche) accompagné par deux de ses amies, très excitées.

PAUL FENTON/SHOOTING STAR/COLORIFIC!

Husbands and wives and adopted daughters. (Above) Mia Farrow at the time of the custody hearing in which she alleged that Woody Allen (opposite, left) had sexually abused her adopted daughter Dylan, 25 August 1992. In December 1997, Allen married Soon-Yi Previn (opposite, right), another of Farrow's adopted children...

Ehemänner und Ehefrauen – und Adoptivtöchter. (Oben) Mia Farrow zur Zeit des Sorgerechts-Streits um ihre und Woody Allens (gegenüberliegende Seite, links) gemeinsame Adoptivtochter Dylan, 25. August 1992. Farrow beschuldigte Allen des sexuellen Missbrauchs an Dylan. Im Dezember 1997 heiratete Allen Soon-Yi Previn (gegenüberliegende Seite, rechts), eine weitere Adoptivtochter von Farrow ...

Maris, femmes et filles adoptives. (Ci-dessus) Mia Farrow à l'époque du procès où elle avait prétendu que Woody Allen (ci-contre, à gauche) avait abusé sexuellement de sa fille adoptive Dylan, le 25 août 1992. En décembre 1997, Allen épousait Soon-Yi Previn (ci-contre, à droite), une autre fille adoptive de Mia ...

Lolo Ferrari, Cannes Film Festival, 1995. Reluctant porn star Lolo died of 'natural causes' five years later.

Lolo Ferrari beim 1995er Filmfestival von Cannes. Die zurückhaltende Pornodarstellerin starb fünf Jahre später eines „natürlichen Todes".

Lolo Ferrari au Festival de Cannes 1995. Vedette porno à contrecœur, elle décéda de « cause naturelle » cinq ans plus tard.

DEREK W RIDGERS/PYMCA

Pamela Anderson, prominent star of the TV series *Baywatch*, and her husband Tommy Lee at the opening of the Hard Rock Hotel, Las Vegas. Tommy was a member of heavy metal band Motley Crüe.

Pamela Anderson, berühmt-berüchtigter Star der TV-Serie *Baywatch* und ihr Mann Tommy Lee bei der Eröffnung des Hard Rock Hotel in Las Vegas. Tommy war Mitglied der Heavy-Metal-Band Motley Crüe.

Pamela Anderson, éminente vedette de la série télé *Alerte à Malibu*, et son mari Tommy Lee à l'inauguration du Hard Rock Hotel de Las Vegas. Tommy faisait partie du groupe de rock heavy metal Motley Crüe.

RON DAVIS/SHOOTING STAR/COLORIFIC!

Canadian film director David Cronenberg in defensive mode after his screen adaptation of William Burroughs' novel *The Naked Lunch* in 1992. Among Cronenberg's other films of the 1990s were *Crash* and *Existenz*.

Der kanadische Filmregisseur David Cronenberg in Verteidigungshaltung nach seiner filmischen Adaption des Romans von William Burroughs *The Naked Lunch*, 1992. Zu den weiteren Filmen Cronenbergs in den neunziger Jahren gehörten *Crash* und *Existenz*.

Le réalisateur canadien David Cronenberg adopte une attitude défensive après *Le Festin nu*, son adaptation à l'écran du roman de William Burroughs en 1992. *Crash* et *Existenz* comptent parmi ses autres films des années 1990.

American film director and actor Spike Jonze, December 1999. Jonze cut his film teeth on highly original pop videos, and went on the make the successful *Being John Malkovich*.

Der amerikanische Schauspieler und Regisseur Spike Jonze im Dezember 1999. Jonze verdiente sich erste Sporen mit höchst originellen Popvideos, bevor er mit *Being John Malkovich* einen Kinoerfolg landete.

Le réalisateur et acteur Spike Jonze, en décembre 1999. Jonze se fit d'abord les dents sur des vidéos pop très originales avant de se lancer dans la réalisation de *Dans la peau de John Malkovich*.

CHERYL DUNN/VISAGES/COLORIFIC!

Mr and Mrs Francis Ford Coppola (centre and left respectively) with their daughter Sofia, on a family night out in Hollywood. Sofia Coppola made her directorial debut in 1998 with *The Virgin Suicides*.

Mr. und Mrs. Francis Ford Coppola (Mitte und links) mit ihrer Tochter Sofia bei einem nächtlichen Familienausflug in Hollywood. Sofia Coppola gab 1998 mit *The Virgin Suicides* ihr Regiedebüt.

Monsieur et madame Francis Ford Coppola (au centre et à gauche) avec leur fille Sofia lors d'une sortie en famille à Hollywood. Sofia Coppola fit ses débuts de réalisatrice en 1998 avec *The Virgin Suicides*.

John Malkovich savours success, 1997. He was the eponymous star of the 1999 movie *Being John Malkovich*.

John Malkovich genießt den Erfolg, 1997. Malkovich war gleichzeitig Hauptdarsteller und Namensgeber des Films *Being John Malkovich* von 1999.

John Malkovich savoure le succès en 1997. Il était la vedette éponyme du film *Dans la peau de John Malkovich* (1999).

HOWARD ROSENBERG/SHOOTING STAR/COLORIFIC!

Gérard Depardieu is dusted with confetti after receiving the Tele-Tydzien award in Warsaw for best foreign actor of 1999.

Gérard Depardieu im Konfettiregen nach der Entgegennahme des polnischen Tele-Tydzien-Preises für den besten ausländischen Schauspieler, Warschau, 1999.

Gérard Depardieu sous une pluie de confettis après avoir reçu le prix Tele-Tydzien du meilleur acteur étranger de 1999, à Varsovie.

STEFAN ROUSSEAU/PA

Tom Cruise and Nicole Kidman arrive in St Albans, Hertfordshire,
for the funeral of the film director Stanley Kubrick, 12 March 1999.
Both had recently filmed *Eyes Wide Shut* with Kubrick.

Tom Cruise und Nicole Kidman auf dem Weg zur Beisetzung Stanley
Kubricks in St. Albans, Hertfordshire, am 12. März 1999. Kurz zuvor
hatten beide noch mit Kubrick den Film *Eyes Wide Shut* gedreht.

Tom Cruise et Nicole Kidman arrivent à St Albans (Hertfordshire)
pour les funérailles du réalisateur britannique Stanley Kubrick,
le 12 mars 1999, dont ils venaient de tourner tous deux *Eyes Wide Shut*.

Brad Pitt and
Gwyneth Paltrow
chill out on Bleeker
Street, Greenwich
Village, New York,
15 June 1995.

Brad Pitt und
Gwyneth Paltrow
entspannen sich
auf der Bleeker
Street in Greenwich
Village, New York,
15. Juni 1995.

Brad Pitt et
Gwyneth Paltrow
se détendent dans
Bleeker Street, à
Greenwich Village
(New York),
le 15 juin 1995.

Meanwhile, in another part of town... Warren Beatty on location for *Town and Country*, 15 September 1998.

Inzwischen, in einem anderen Stadtteil ... Warren Beatty bei den Dreharbeiten zu *Town and Country,* 15. September 1998.

Dans un autre quartier de la ville ... Warren Beatty sur le tournage de *Town and Country,* le 15 septembre 1998.

CHRIS BACON/PA

Rising stars. (Left) Mel Gibson's Highland spring at the MacRobert Arts Centre, Stirling, before the premiere of *Braveheart*, 3 September 1995. (Opposite) Roberto Benigni sweeps Helen Hunt off her feet as he celebrates his Screen Actors Guild Award, 8 March 1999.

Stars auf dem Sprung. (Links) Mel Gibson 'high' in den Highlands beim MacRoberts Arts Centre in Stirling, Schottland, vor der Premiere von *Braveheart*, 3. September 1995. (Gegenüberliegende Seite) Roberto Benigni holt zur Feier des Tages Helen Hunt von den Beinen. Gerade wurde ihm der Screen Actors Guild Award verliehen, 8. März 1999.

Des stars montantes. (À gauche) Le saut écossais de Mel Gibson au MacRobert Arts Centre de Stirling avant la première de *Braveheart*, le 3 septembre 1995. (Ci-contre) Roberto Benigni soulève Helen Hunt de plaisir en apprenant qu'il a été récompensé par le Screen Actors Guild Award, le 8 mars 1999.

American actor
Harvey Keitel,
who played the
part of Mr White
in Mr Tarantino's
Reservoir Dogs.

Der amerikanische
Schauspieler Harvey
Keitel, der die Rolle
des Mr. White in
Mr. Tarantinos
Reservoir Dogs
spielte.

L'acteur américain
Harvey Keitel,
qui jouait le rôle
de Mr White dans
Reservoir Dogs
de Tarantino.

HOWARD ROSENBERG/SHOOTING STAR/COLORIFIC!

Writer, actor and director Quentin Tarantino. Critics were unsure as to whether or not the violence in films such as *Reservoir Dogs* and *Pulp Fiction* masked a lack of talent or overrode a cinematic genius.

Der Drehbuchautor, Schauspieler und Regisseur Quentin Tarantino. Die Kritiker waren uneins darüber, ob die Gewaltdarstellungen in Filmen wie *Reservoir Dogs* oder *Pulp Fiction* einen Mangel an Talent kaschierten oder das Werk eines filmischen Genies übertrafen.

L'écrivain, acteur et réalisateur Quentin Tarantino. Les critiques se sont demandés si la violence présente dans des films comme *Reservoir Dogs* et *Pulp Fiction* masquait un manque de talent ou avait dépassé un cinéaste de génie.

Actor and director Dennis Hopper, star of many films in the 1990s including *Waterworld* and *True Romance*.

Der Schauspieler und Regisseur Dennis Hopper, Hauptdarsteller zahlreicher Filme in den neunziger Jahren, darunter *Waterworld* und *True Romance*.

L'acteur et réalisateur Dennis Hopper, vedette de nombreux films des années 1990, dont *Waterworld* et *True Romance*.

American film director David Lynch, whose 1990s credits included *Twin Peaks*, *Wild at Heart* and *The Straight Story*.

Der amerikanische Filmregisseur David Lynch, dessen Werk in den neunziger Jahren Filme wie *Twin Peaks*, *Wild at Heart* und *The Straight Story* umfasste.

Le réalisateur américain David Lynch, auteur de films comme *Twin Peaks*, *Sailor et Lula* et *Une Histoire vraie*.

ANTHONY BARBOZA/SHOOTING STAR/COLORIFIC!

6. The Arts
Kunst
Les arts

Damien Hirst and his assistants prepare some of his work for Expo 1996 at the Gogosian Gallery, New York City. Hirst was the ageing *enfant terrible* of British art during the 1990s.

Damien Hirst und seine Assistenten bereiten eine seiner Arbeiten für die Expo 1996 in der Gogosian Gallery, New York City, vor. Hirst war das alternde Enfant terrible der britischen Kunst in den neunziger Jahren.

Damien Hirst et ses assistants préparent certaines des œuvres qu'il présentera à l'Expo 1996 de la galerie Gogosian de New York. Hirst fut l'enfant terrible vieillissant de l'art britannique pendant les années 1990.

6. The Arts
   Kunst
   Les arts

The shock tactics employed by angry young artists towards the end of the 1980s were pressed home *ad infinitum* throughout the 1990s. Paint and canvas, pencil and paper disappeared from the walls of galleries and art houses world-wide, to be replaced by structures, whole rooms and even entire houses in the guise of artistic creations. The proliferation of awards and prizes was seen by some as simply a way of indulging the glitterati, who flocked to presentation ceremonies in clothes as outlandish as the exhibits themselves.

The novel continued to die as an art form, as, it was claimed, it had been doing for well over half a century. Novelists took little notice of its alleged terminal condition. Salman Rushdie spent much of the decade in hiding from the *fatwa* imposed upon him in 1989. Martin Amis spent less time hiding from his dentist. Tom Wolfe wrote very little.

The Royal Opera House in London struggled to survive a series of financial and managerial crises, though opera and ballet had never before been so popular. A cad blew the whistle on price fixing by the leading auction houses, but all was quickly smoothed over. It was, as ever, a case of 'art for art's sake, but money, for God's sake!'

Die Schockeffekte, auf die zornige junge Künstler gegen Ende der achtziger Jahre zunehmend setzten, wurden in den neunziger Jahren schier endlos ausgereizt. Farbe und Leinwand, Stift und Papier verschwanden von den Wänden der Galerien und Museen der Welt. An ihrer Stelle wurden Strukturen, ganze Räume und sogar komplette Gebäude unter dem Deckmantel künstlerischen Schaffens präsentiert. Die Inflation an Preisen und Auszeichnungen erschien vielen nur als Vehikel der Schickeria, sich selbst zu feiern und in Scharen zu Vernissagen und Präsentationen zu strömen – meist in Kleider gewandet, die den Kunstwerken in puncto Seltsamkeit in nichts nachstand.

Der Roman als Kunstform setzte sein langsames Sterben fort, das für manche bereits vor über einem halben Jahrhundert eingesetzt hatte. Die Romanciers freilich kümmerte ihr angebliches Endstadium herzlich wenig. Salman Rushdie verbrachte den Großteil des Jahrzehnts an geheimen Orten, versteckt vor der Fatwa, die man 1989 über ihn verhängt hatte. Martin Amis versteckte sich weniger vor seinem Zahnarzt. Tom Wolfe schrieb wenig.

Das Londoner Royal Opera House kämpfte inmitten einer Reihe von Finanz- und Führungskrisen ums Überleben, obwohl Ballett und Oper so populär wie nie zuvor waren. Ein übel meinender Zeitgenosse verbot die Absprachen von Höchstpreisen seitens der führenden Auktionshäuser. Aber auch diese Wogen sollten sich schnell glätten. Wie immer verbargen sich hinter dem Motto „Kunst um der Kunst Willen" nicht selten finanzielle Interessen.

Les tactiques de choc employées par de jeunes artistes en colère vers la fin des années 1980 furent prolongées ad infinitum pendant les années 1990. Peinture et toile, crayon et papier disparurent des cimaises des galeries d'art et des musées du monde entier pour être remplacés par des créations artistiques sous forme d'installations, de salles ou de maisons entières. La prolifération des récompenses et des prix était considérée par certains comme un moyen simple de faire plaisir aux membres de la bonne société, qui se précipitaient d'ailleurs aux vernissages dans des costumes au moins aussi étranges que les œuvres exposées.

Le roman continuait d'agoniser en tant que forme d'art mais cela faisait déjà plus d'un demi-siècle qu'on annonçait sa mort sans que les romanciers eux-mêmes en tiennent vraiment compte. Salman Rushdie vécut caché une grande partie de la décennie pour échapper à la fatwa lancée contre lui en 1989. Martin Amis passa moins de temps à échapper à son dentiste. Tom Wolfe écrivit très peu.

La Royal Opera House de Londres luttait pour survivre après une série de crises financières et directoriales, bien que l'opéra et le ballet n'aient jamais été aussi populaires. Un malotru dénonça la fixation des cours par les principales charges de vente aux enchères avant que tout ne soit rapidement étouffé. Comme toujours, c'était « l'art pour l'amour de l'art, et l'argent pour l'amour de Dieu ! »

Inspired by illness, Tracey Emin's *My Bed* is shown to the press at the Turner Prize Exhibition, Tate Gallery, London, 19 October 1999.

Krankheit als Inspiration. Tracey Emins Werk *My Bed* bei der Pressevorführung im Rahmen der Turner-Prize-Ausstellung in der Londoner Tate Gallery, 19. Oktober 1999.

Inspiré par la maladie, *My Bed* de Tracey Emin est présenté à la presse lors de la Turner Prize Exhibition, à la Tate Gallery de Londres, le 19 octobre 1999.

EPA/PA

The scene is the Brooklyn Museum of Art, 30 September 1999. In the foreground is Damien Hirst's *The Physical Impossibility of Death in the Mind of Someone Living*. In the background is Marcus Harvey's portrait of Myra Hindley.

Brooklyn Museum of Art, 30. September 1999. Im Vordergrund Damien Hirsts *The Physical Impossibility of Death in the Mind of Someone Living* (Die physische Unmöglichkeit des Todes in den Gedanken eines Lebenden), im Hintergrund sieht man Marcus Harveys Porträt von Myra Hindley.

La scène se passe au Brooklyn Museum of Art, le 30 septembre 1999. On reconnaît au premier plan une œuvre de Damien Hirst – *The Physical Impossibility of Death in the Mind of Someone Living* – et, au fond, le portrait de Myra Hindley par Marcus Harvey.

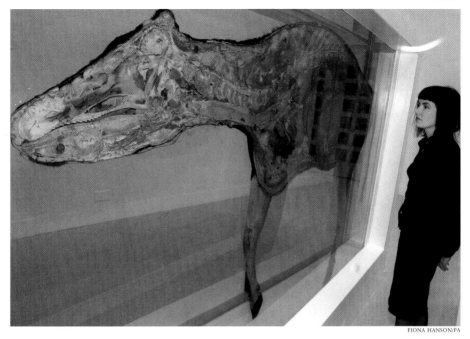

FIONA HANSON/PA

Much of Damien Hirst's work in the 1990s exhibited the versatility of formaldehyde. *Mother and Child Divided* (above), at the Tate Gallery, contained a bisected cow and calf. The Brooklyn work (opposite) contained a piece of tiger shark.

Ein großer Teil von Damien Hirsts Arbeiten in den neunziger Jahren stellte vor allem die Vielseitigkeit von Formaldehyd aus. *Mother and Child Divided* (Mutter und Kind getrennt, oben) in der Tate Gallery bestand aus einer halbierten Kuh mitsamt Kalb. Die Arbeit aus Brooklyn (gegenüberliegende Seite) enthielt Teile eines Tigerhais.

Une grande partie des œuvres des années 1990 de Damien Hirst démontrait la souplesse d'utilisation du formol. *Mother and Child Divided* (ci-dessus), à la Tate Gallery, contenait une vache pleine (avec son veau) coupée en deux. L'œuvre présentée à Brooklyn (ci-contre) présentait un morceau de requin tigre.

HARTMUT REEH/EPA/PA

An exhibit by the Japanese artist Fukuichi Yoshida at the Paper Art 7 show in the Leopold-Hoesch-Museum, Düren, Germany, 3 September 1998. The work covers the floor of a room with bags folded from Japanese paper.

Eine Arbeit der japanischen Künstlerin Fukuichi Yoshida im Rahmen der Paper Art 7 im Dürener Leopold-Hoesch-Museum, 3. September 1998. Die Raum-installation bestand aus einer Reihe gefalteter Behälter aus Japanpapier, die den gesamten Boden bedeckten.

Une exposition de l'artiste japonais Fukuichi Yoshida au Paper Art 7 du Leopold-Hoesch-Museum de Düren (Allemagne), le 3 septembre 1998. L'installation se compose d'une multitude de sacs en papier japonais.

TORSTEN BLACKWOOD/PA

British artist Martin Creed peers out above the sea of 43,000 white balloons that make up his exhibit *Half the Air in a Given Space*, Goat Island, Sydney Harbour, Australia, 16 September 1998.

Der britische Künstler Martin Creed lugt aus einem Meer von 43 000 weißen Luftballons hervor, aus denen sein Werk *Half the Air in a Given Space* (Die halbe Menge Luft in einem gegebenen Raum) bestand. Goat Island, Hafen von Sydney, Australien, 16. September 1998.

L'artiste britannique Martin Creed émerge de la mer des 43 000 ballons blancs de son installation – *Half the Air in a Given Space* –, créée à Goat Island, dans le port de Sydney (Australie), le 16 septembre 1998.

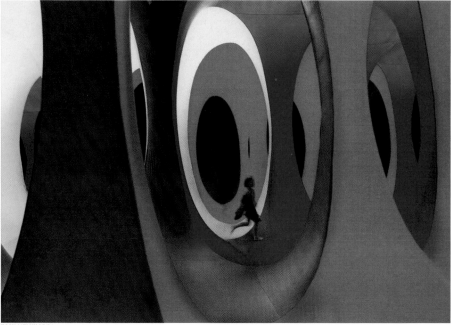

TOBY MELVILLE/PA

Confronting space. Visitors explore Maurice Agis's *Dreamspace*, a giant inflatable work of art and the largest pneumatic creation in the world, Mile End Park, east London, 15 July 1999.

Konfrontation im Raum. Besucher im Mile End Park im Osten Londons erkunden Maurice Agis' *Dreamspace* (Traum-Raum), ein überdimensionales, aufblasbares Kunstwerk und gleichzeitig das weltweit größte pneumatische Objekt, 15. Juli 1999.

Affronter l'espace. Des visiteurs explorent *Dreamspace,* une gigantesque œuvre gonflable de Maurice Agis et la plus grande création pneumatique du monde, installée à Mile End Park, à l'est de Londres, le 15 juillet 1999.

FIONA HANSON/PA

Contemplating space. Andrea Davis clasps her head in wonder at one of Simon Patterson's submissions for the Turner Prize, Tate Gallery, London, 28 October 1996.

Nachdenken über den Raum. Andrea Davis rauft sich ungläubig die Haare angesichts von Simon Pattersons Wettbewerbsbeitrag um dem Turner Prize, Tate Gallery, London, 28. Oktober 1996.

Contempler l'espace. Andrea Davis se tient la tête d'admiration devant l'une des soumissions de Simon Patterson pour le Turner Prize, à la Tate Gallery (Londres), le 28 octobre 1996.

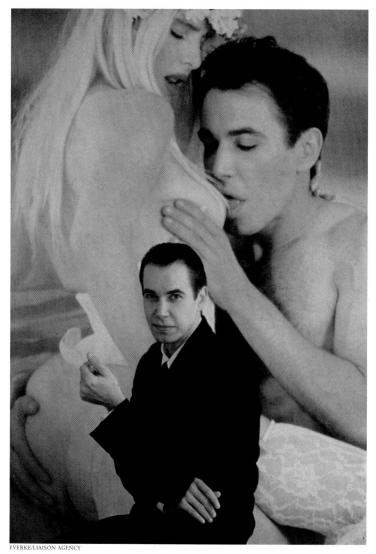

Jeff Koons sits in front of a portrait of himself and his wife, La Cicciolina, for the X-Rated Art Show, 21 November 1991.

Jeff Koons vor einem Porträt, das ihn mit seiner Frau La Cicciolina zeigt. Die Aufnahme entstand im Rahmen der Ausstellung X-Rated Art Show, 21. November 1991.

Jeff Koons est assis devant un portrait le représentant avec sa femme, La Cicciolina, lors du X-Rated Art Show, le 21 novembre 1991.

Another medium, another icon. Jeff Koons's sculpture of Michael Jackson and his pet monkey, Bubbles, 8 December 1999. The work was part of the 'Heaven' exhibition at the Tate Gallery, Liverpool.

Ein anderes Material und eine andere Ikone. Jeff Koons' Skulptur von Michael Jackson und seinem Affen Bubbles, 8. Dezember 1999. Das Werk war Teil der Ausstellung Heaven in der Liverpooler Tate Gallery.

Autre médium, autre icône. La statue de Michael Jackson et de son singe par Jeff Koons, exposée à Bubbles, le 8 décembre 1999. L'œuvre faisait partie de l'exposition « Heaven » à la Tate Gallery de Liverpool.

Since 1972
Christo Javacheff
had been planning
to wrap the
Reichstag in Berlin.
He finally achieved
his ambition in
June 1995.

Seit 1972 plante
Christo Javacheff,
den Berliner Reichs-
tag zu verpacken.
Im Juni 1995
schließlich ging sein
Traum in Erfüllung.

Christo Javacheff
rêvait d'emballer
le Reichstag de
Berlin depuis 1972.
Il put enfin réaliser
son ambition
en juin 1995.

Dancing feet. American dancer, choreographer and founder of her own company, Twyla Tharp poses for the camera.

Tanzende Füße. Die amerikanische Tänzerin, Choreografin und Gründerin ihres eigenen Ensembles Twyla Tharp posiert für die Kamera.

Des pieds pour danser. L'américaine Twyla Tharp, danseuse, choré-graphe et fondatrice de sa compagnie de ballet, pose devant l'objectif.

GREG GORMAN/LIAISON AGENCY

Defending hands. US artist Julian Schnabel, painter and printmaker, best known for such works as *Portrait of José Luis Ferrer*.

Abwehrende Hände. Der amerikanische Maler und Grafiker Julian Schnabel, bekannt unter anderem für sein Werk *Portrait of José Luis Ferrer*.

Des mains pour se défendre. L'artiste, peintre et graveur américain Julian Schnabel est plus connu pour des œuvres comme *Portrait of José Luis Ferrer*.

STUDIO VALLETOUX/MPA/LIAISON AGENCY

The dance goes on. A pirouetting portrait of the English ballerina Darcy Bussell.

Der Tanz geht weiter. Ein Porträt der englischen Ballerina Darcy Bussell beim Drehen einer Pirouette.

Figure de danse. Une pirouette décomposée de la ballerine anglaise Darcy Bussell.

FRANCOIS DARMIGNY/SAOLA/COLORIFIC!

Emerging from his hideout, Salman Rushdie views the 1990s literary scene. His works from the decade included *Haroun and the Sea of Dreams*, *The Moor's Last Sigh*, *The Ground Beneath Her Feet* and *East, West*.

Von seinem Versteck aus beobachtet Salman Rushdie die literarische Szene der neunziger Jahre. Zu seinen Werken in dieser Dekade zählen *Harun und das Meer der Geschichten*, *Des Mauren letzter Seufzer*, *Der Boden unter ihren Füßen* und *Osten, Westen*.

Émergeant de sa cachette, Salman Rushdie contemple la scène littéraire des années 1990. *Haroun et la mer des histoires*, *Le Dernier Soupir du Maure*, *La Terre sous ses pieds* et *Est, Ouest* comptent parmi ses œuvres publiées dans la décennie.

Mouth wide shut. Martin Amis risks *Time's Arrow* on his way to (much earlier) *Success* in *London Fields*.

Den Mund weit geschlossen. Martin Amis blickt auf seine Erfolge zurück. Dazu zählen die Romane *Erfolg*, *London Fields* und *Der Pfeil der Zeit*.

La bouche grande fermée. Martin Amis risque *La Flèche du temps* en route vers le *Success* (bien antérieur) dans les *London Fields*.

KAI PFAFFENBACH/REUTERS/ARCHIVE PHOTOS

Günter Grass (left) clasps the hand of Turkish author Yasar Kemal after the latter had been awarded the Peace Prize of the German Book Trade at the Frankfurt Book Fair, 19 October 1997.

Günter Grass (links) drückt die Hand des türkischen Autors Yasar Kemal, nachdem Letzterer auf der Frankfurter Buchmesse mit dem Friedenspreis des Deutschen Buchhandels ausgezeichnet wurde, 19. Oktober 1997.

Günter Grass (à gauche) serre la main de l'auteur turc Yasar Kemal après que ce dernier a obtenu le prix de la Paix décerné par le Cercle des Libraires allemands au Salon du livre de Francfort, le 19 octobre 1997.

Nobel prize-winning author Gabriel Garcia Marquez doffs his hat to a left-wing freedom fighter in San Vicente del Caguan, Colombia, 7 January 1999. The writer was on his way to take part in peace talks.

Der Nobelpreisträger und Autor Gabriel Garcia Marquez zieht seinen Hut vor einem linksgerichteten Freiheitskämpfer in San Vicente del Caguan, Kolumbien, 7. Januar 1999. Der Autor sollte an Friedensgesprächen teilnehmen.

Gabriel Garcia Marquez, lauréat du prix Nobel de littérature, tient son chapeau en passant devant un combattant de la liberté à San Vicente del Caguan, le 7 janvier 1999, où l'écrivain devait participer à des conférences sur la paix.

English actor, producer, playwright and film director David Hare takes a view from the stalls.

Der englische Schauspieler, Produzent, Dramatiker und Regisseur David Hare nimmt die Perspektive der Zuschauer ein.

L'acteur, producteur, scénariste et réalisateur anglais David Hare installé dans la salle de projection.

American playwright and film director David Mamet on the set of his film *Homicide*, 1991. Among his most successful works in the 1990s were *Glengarry Glen Ross*, *American Buffalo* and *Wag the Dog*.

Der amerikanische Drehbuchautor und Regisseur David Mamet am Set zu seinem Film *Homicide*, 1991. Zu seinen erfolgreichsten Werken in den neunziger Jahren zählten *Glengarry Glen Ross, American Buffalo – das Glück liegt auf der Straße* und *Wag the Dog – wenn der Schwanz mit dem Hund wedelt.*

Le scénariste et réalisateur américain David Mamet sur le tournage de son film *Homicide,* en 1991. Ses œuvres les plus appréciées des années 1990 furent *L'Affaire Glengarry, American Buffalo* et *Des Hommes d'influence.*

MAX RAMIREZ/BLACK STAR/COLORIFIC!

Cyberpunks, 1994. The phenomenon was created by the writer
William Gibson (opposite), and the image was a weird mixture of
punk, sci-fi, martial arts, soft drinks and the whole world of cyberspace.

Cyberpunks 1994. Der Autor William Gibson (gegenüberliegende Seite)
erfand ihre Welt – eine seltsame Mischung aus Punk, Kampfkunst,
Science-Fiction, Softdrinks und der virtuellen Realität des Cyberspace.

Cyberpunks, 1994. Ce phénomène, créé par l'écrivain William Gibson
(ci-contre), mélange curieusement l'esprit punk, la science-fiction, les
arts martiaux, les boissons sans alcool et tout le monde du Cyberspace.

William Gibson, creator of the *Sprawl* series that included *Neuromancer*, *Count Zero* and *Mona Lisa Overdrive*.

William Gibson, Autor der Neuromancer-Trilogie bestehend aus den Romanen *Neuromancer, Biochips* und *Mona Lisa Overdrive*.

William Gibson, créateur de la série culte *Sprawl*, composée de *Neuromancien, Comte Zéro* et *Mona Lisa s'éclate*.

EXLEY/LIAISON AGENCY

7. Pop
Pop
Pop

Keeping the flame of the 1980s alive, the American shock rocker
Marilyn Manson ignites his Paris audience, 19 December 1998.

Das Feuer der 1980er brennt weiter in Person des amerikanischen
Schockrockers Marilyn Manson, der hier sein Pariser Publikum
entflammt, 19. Dezember 1998.

Entretenant la flamme des années 1980, le stupéfiant rocker américain
Marilyn Manson embrase son public parisien, le 19 décembre 1998.

7. Pop
Pop
Pop

In the ever more frantic business of pop it now took too long to discover 'talent'. Better by far for promoters and record companies to identify a niche in the market, set up a publicity machine, and then create a star band or singer from scratch. And the younger such fledgling stars could be fed into the system, the longer their careers might last. Some were all too ephemeral, but Stepz, Boyzone, Westlife and the Spice Girls were all accorded veteran status after a couple of years at the top.

There were still hard-faced, hard-line rockers on the circuit, but the new fashion was for a clean-cut image. Britney Spears tapped into the planet's thirst for morality by flaunting her virginity. The Spice Girls insisted in song that 'if you want to be my lover, you gotta get with my friends…' Michael Jackson, who reached the age of forty in 1998, was rumoured to have sinned, and his career suffered accordingly. Madonna, meanwhile, steered an erratic but successful course between propriety and impropriety.

It was okay to be gay, and Queen superstar Freddie Mercury passed into the All Time Rock 'n' Roll Hall of Fame with his death from AIDS in November 1991.

Das zunehmend schnelllebige Popbusiness ließ keine Zeit mehr für die Suche nach echten Talenten. Stattdessen setzten Promoter und Plattenfirmen darauf, eine Marktnische zu finden, die Publicitymaschine in Gang zu setzen und schließlich aus dem Nichts eine Band oder einen Popstar zu erschaffen. Und je eher solche gerade einmal flüggen Popstars dem System zugeführt werden konnten, desto größer die Chance auf eine lange Karriere. Einige dieser Karrieren stellten sich als allzu kurzlebig heraus, andere Bands allerdings, wie die Stepz, Boyzone, Westlife oder die Spice Girls erreichten schon nach ein paar Jahren an der Spitze den Status von „Veteranen".

Nach wie vor gab es die harten Rocker mit ihren harten Gesichtern, doch die Mode verlangte nach sauberen, scharf umrissenen Images. Britney Spears stillte den Hunger des Planeten nach Moral, indem sie mit ihrer Jungfräulichkeit hausieren ging. Die Spice Girls bestanden in einem ihrer Hits darauf: „Wenn du mein Liebhaber sein willst/musst du zuerst mein Freund werden". Michael Jackson, der 1998 seinen 40. Geburtstag feierte, sollte Gerüchten zufolge „gesündigt" haben, was seiner Karriere nicht unerheblichen Schaden zufügte. Währenddessen steuerte Madonna einen unberechenbaren und gleichsam erfolgreichen Kurs zwischen Schicklichkeit und Skandal.

Schwulsein wurde akzeptiert – wie im Falle des Superstars von Queen Freddie Mercury, der nach seinem Tod durch das Aidsvirus im November 1991 in die Ruhmeshalle des Rock 'n' Roll aufgenommen wurde.

Il fallait désormais trop de temps pour découvrir et exploiter un véritable « talent » dans le monde toujours mouvant de la musique pop. Pour les promoteurs et les compagnies de disque, il était plus facile d'identifier une niche sur le marché, de lancer un battage publicitaire puis de créer ex nihilo un groupe ou un chanteur. Et plus ces stars débutantes sont intégrées jeunes dans le système, plus leur carrière peut durer longtemps. Si certains eurent une vie plus qu'éphémère, des groupes comme Stepz, Boyzone, Westlife ou les Spice Girls obtinrent tous le titre de vétéran après avoir passé quelques années au sommet des charts.

Si les rockers purs et durs restaient dans le circuit, la nouvelle mode était celle d'une image plus « clean ». Britney Spears jouait sur le besoin de moralité de la planète en proclamant sa virginité. Les Spice Girls en rajoutaient en chantant « si tu veux être mon amour, sois d'abord mon ami… » Une rumeur ayant accusé de péché Michael Jackson, qui atteignait l'âge de quarante ans en 1998, sa carrière en subit les conséquences. Madonna, entre-temps, poursuivait une carrière erratique – mais couronnée de succès – entre bienséance et inconvenance.

Il était bien vu d'être gay, Freddie Mercury, la superstar du groupe Queen, entre au Panthéon du Rock éternel en décédant du Sida en novembre 1991.

Unmoved, a security
guard protects
Boyzone during
the *Smash Hits*
1995 Poll Winners
Party, London,
3 December 1995.

Sichtlich regungslos
bewacht dieser
Sicherheitsmann den
Auftritt der Gruppe
Boyzone auf einer
Party des englischen
Musikmagazins
Smash Hits, bei der
die Sieger der jähr-
lichen Leserumfrage
auftraten, London,
3. Dezember 1995.

Indifférent, un agent
de sécurité protège
les membres de
Boyzone lors des
Smash Hits de la
Poll Winners Party
1995 à Londres,
le 3 décembre 1995.

Oh, brother…
Michael Jackson in
full flow, HIStory
World Tour, Prague,
7 September 1996.

Oh Bruder …
Michael Jackson
in seinem Element
während der
HIStory-Welt-
tournee, Prag,
7. September 1996.

Oh, brother…
Michael Jackson en
plein élan pendant
son HIStory World
Tour à Prague, le
7 septembre 1996.

Oh, sister… Janet
Jackson at full stretch
in the Sheffield
Arena, Yorkshire,
April 1995.

Oh Schwester …
Janet Jackson steht
ihrem Bruder in
nichts nach, Sheffield
Arena, Yorkshire,
April 1995.

Oh, sister… Janet
Jackson en plein
effort sur la scène
de la Sheffield Arena
(Yorkshire),
en avril 1995.

ANTONY MEDLEY/S.I.N.

A pregnant Melanie
Blatt of All Saints
on stage at the Party
in the Park concert
for the Prince's
Trust, London,
5 July 1998.

Die schwangere
Melanie Blatt von
den All Saints auf
der Bühne beim
Konzert Party in the
Park zu Gunsten der
Stiftung von Prinz
Charles, London,
5. Juli 1998.

Melanie Blatt, des
All Saints, enceinte,
sur scène pour le
concert Party in
the Park à l'occasion
du Prince's Trust,
à Londres,
le 5 juillet 1998.

STEFAN ROUSSEAU/PA

Robbie Williams (left) and Tom Jones duet at the Brit Awards, London Docklands Arena, 9 February 1998. Williams was romantically linked with another of All Saints, Natalie Appleton.

Robbie Williams (links) und Tom Jones bei einem Duett im Rahmen der Brit Awards in der Londoner Docklands Arena, 9. Februar 1998. Williams hatte eine Affäre mit Natalie Appleton, einem anderen Mitglied der All Saints.

Robbie Williams (à gauche) et Tom Jones chantent en duo aux Brit Awards, organisé au London Docklands Arena, le 9 février 1998. Williams avait une liaison romantique avec Natalie Appleton, une autre chanteuse des All Saints.

COLORIFIC!

Britney Spears enjoys a playback in 1998, the year her career took off. Following her Month in the Malls promotional tour, she released *Baby, One More Time*. The rest was instant history.

Britney Spears freut sich über ein Playback. Das Bild entstand 1998, dem Jahr, in dem ihre Karriere startete. Nach ihrer Promotiontour Month in the Malls erschien *Baby, One More Time*. Der Rest wurde augenblicklich Geschichte.

Britney Spears s'amuse en se réécoutant en 1998, l'année où sa carrière a décollé. Après sa tournée de promotion, Month in the Malls, elle enregistrait *Baby, One More Time*. La suite appartient à l'histoire immédiate.

A promotional shot of the Spice Girls for their 1997 movie *Spiceworld*. They were then at the height of their fame and success.

Ein Promotionfoto der Spice Girls für ihren Film *Spiceworld*, 1997. Zu diesem Zeitpunkt befand sich die Gruppe auf dem Höhepunkt ihres Erfolgs.

Une photo promotionnelle des Spice Girls à l'occasion de la sortie en 1997 de leur film *Spiceworld*. Elles étaient alors au summum de leur célébrité et de leur réussite.

LINDSAY BRICE/VISAGES/COLORIFIC!

The fan who headed for the stars… Part of the audience at a Sonic Youth gig, 1992. They made their name with *Bad Moon Rising* in the late 1980s, and became one of the first alternative bands to hit the big time in the early 1990s.

Der Fan, der nach den „Sternen" griff … Ein Teil des Publikums bei einem Sonic-Youth-Auftritt des Jahres 1992. In den späten achtziger Jahren machte sich die Band mit *Bad Moon Rising* einen Namen und landete als eine der ersten „alternativen" Bands große Erfolge in den frühen neunziger Jahren.

Des fans à la rencontre de leurs stars… Une partie du public lors d'un concert des Sonic Youth en 1992. Ils se firent connaître à la fin des années 1980 grâce à *Bad Moon Rising*, et devinrent l'un des premiers groupes alternatifs à avoir du succès au début des années 1990.

Sonic Youth on stage at the same concert. It was the year they released their pop-oriented hit album *Dirty*. Ahead lay *A Thousand Leaves* (1998) and *NYC Ghosts and Flowers* (2000).

Sonic Youth auf der Bühne beim selben Konzert. 1992 war das Jahr, in dem sie ihr Pop-orientiertes Album *Dirty* auf den Markt brachten. Es folgten *A Thousand Leaves* (1998) und *NYC Ghosts and Flowers* (2000).

Sonic Youth sur scène lors du même concert. Ils sortirent cette année-là *Dirty*, un album d'inspiration pop, que suivirent *Thousand Leaves* (1998) et *NYC Ghosts and Flowers* (2000).

MICK HUTSON/IDOLS

The perils of pop… Noel Gallagher of Oasis left
the band three times in the 1990s. He blamed his
brother Liam's drinking habits for the repeated splits.

Pop-Gefahren … Noel Gallagher von Oasis verließ
die Band in den neunziger Jahren drei Mal, jeweils
wegen der Trinkgelage seines Bruders Liam.

Les dangers de la pop … Noel Gallagher quitta trois
fois le groupe Oasis dans les années 1990. Il reprochait
à son frère Liam d'être trop porté sur la boisson.

The tragedy of pop... Kurt Cobain of grunge band Nirvana and his wife Courtney Love of Hole. Cobain killed himself, leaving a note which ended: 'Please keep going, Courtney... I love you, I love you.'

Pop-Tragödien ... Kurt Cobain von der Grunge-Band Nirvana und seine Frau Courtney Love, Sängerin der Gruppe Hole. Cobain beging Selbstmord. Sein Abschiedsbrief endete mit den Worten: „Bitte halt durch, Courtney ... Ich liebe Dich, ich liebe Dich."

La tragédie de la pop ... Kurt Cobain, du groupe grunge Nirvana, et sa femme Courtney Love du groupe Hole. Cobain se suicida en laissant un mot qui finissait par : « Continue, Courtney ... Je t'aime, je t'aime ».

P J Harvey discovers the joys of dressing up, earning herself the label 'indie-Madonna' along the way.

P. J. Harvey findet Gefallen daran, sich in Schale zu werfen und verdient sich damit en passant den Titel einer „Independent-Madonna".

P. J. Harvey découvre les joies du déguise-ment, s'attribuant même le titre de la « Madonna indie ».

MARK BENNEY/S.I.N.

Prince reveals his new persona, bearing on his cheeks the self-inflicted labels 'The Artist Formerly Known As Prince' and 'Slave'.

Prince präsentiert seine neue Identität als „The Artist Formerly Known As Prince" („Der Künstler, vormals unter dem Namen Prince bekannt") bzw. als „Slave" („Sklave") – beides hat er sich auf die Wangen gemalt.

Prince révèle son nouveau personnage, où il porte sur les joues les titres autoproclamés de «The Artist Formerly Known As Prince » et « Slave ».

RUSSELL SACH/COLORIFIC!

RICHARD BELAND/S.I.N.

Australian rock star Michael Hutchence of INXS at Marine Terminal 28, 19 November 1993. In an eventful but tragically short life, Hutchence partnered Helena Christensen, Kylie Minogue and Paula Yates before hanging himself in 1997.

Der australische Rockstar Michael Hutchence von der Band INXS im Marine Terminal 28, 19. November 1993. In seinem ereignisreichen wie kurzen Leben war Hutchence mit Helena Christensen, Kylie Minogue und Paula Yates zusammen, bevor er sich im Jahre 1997 erhängte.

La star du rock australien, Michael Hutchence, de INXS, au Marine Terminal 28, le 19 novembre 1993. Malgré une vie trop courte mais riche en rebondissements, il fut le compagnon d'Helena Christensen, de Kylie Minogue et de Paula Yates avant de se pendre en 1997.

Kylie Minogue and
Nick Cave. The two
Australians surprised
everyone by singing
together on the
1996 hit single
*Where the Wild
Roses Grow*.

Kylie Minogue und
Nick Cave. Die
beiden Australier
überraschten die
Popwelt mit ihrem
Duett *Where the
Wild Roses Grow*,
ein Hit aus dem
Jahre 1996.

Kylie Minogue et
Nick Cave. Ces
deux Australiens
surprirent tout le
monde en chantant
en duo en 1996
pour un single :
*Where the Wild
Roses Grow*.

TONY MOTT/S.I.N.

Elvis Costello indulges his eclectic musical tastes while on the go, 1994.

Elvis Costello gibt sich seinen ausgesuchten musikalischen Vorlieben hin – im Gehen, 1994.

Elvis Costello s'abandonne à ses goûts musicaux éclectiques, en 1994.

'It's no secret that ambition bites the nails of success.' Paul Hewson, better known as Bono of U2, here seen expounding on the meaning of 'Pop' during U2's World Tour of 1998.

„Es ist kein Geheimnis, dass Ambitioniertheit und Erfolg sich widersprechen." Paul Hewson, besser bekannt als Bono von U2, entwickelt auf der 1998er Welttournee der Band seine eigene Deutung von „Pop".

«Tout le monde sait que l'ambition ronge les ongles du succès». Paul Hewson, plus connu dans le groupe U2 sous le pseudonyme de Bono, explique le sens de « Pop » lors du World Tour de U2 en 1998.

Lo-fi indie songstress Liz Phair. Her combination of preppy looks and explicit lyrics thrilled the male music establishment.

Die Lo-Fi Independent-Sängerin Liz Phair. Mit ihrer Kombination aus Schulmädchen-Look und anrüchigen Texten versetzte sie das männliche Musik-Establishment in Aufruhr.

La chanteuse indépendante lo-fi Liz Phair, dont l'allure fragile et les textes explicites firent frissonner l'establishment musical masculin.

MAGDA/VISAGES/COLORIFIC!

Hot property from
Iceland. Björk
Gudmundsdottir,
better known simply
as Björk, who
launched her solo
career in 1992.

Heiße Ware aus dem
kalten Island. Björk
Gudmundsdottir,
besser bekannt als
Björk, startete 1992
ihre Solokarriere.

Un volcan d'Islande.
Björk Gudmunds-
dottir, ou plus
simplement Björk,
dont la carrière solo
débuta en 1992.

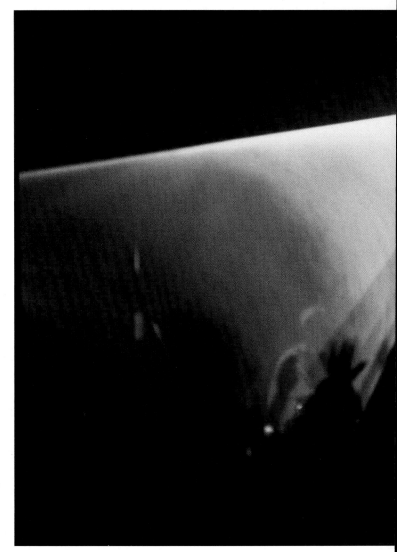

Transcendent pop.
Hands emerge in
silhouette from the
darkness of an acid
house rave.

Transzendenter Pop.
Aus dem Dunkel
eines Acid House
Raves ragen die
Silhouetten von
Händen hervor.

Pop transcendantale.
Des mains émergent
en ombres chinoises
du brouillard
obscur d'une rave
d'acid house.

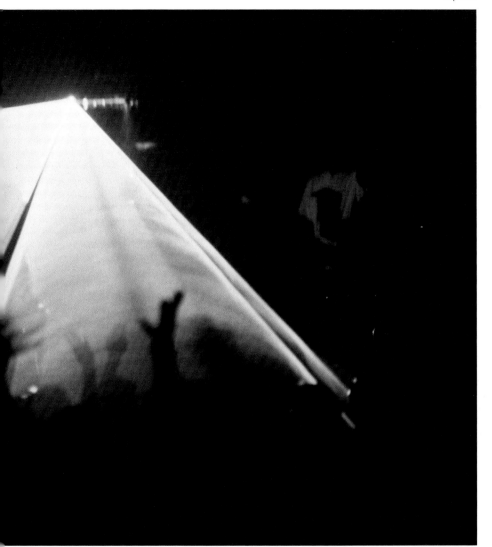

House proud 1. DJ and house music producer Paul Oakenfold, who inaugurated the London super-club Ministry of Sound in the early 1990s.

Bei uns zu House 1. Der DJ und House-Musik-Produzent Paul Oakenfold, der in den frühen neunziger Jahren den Londoner Superclub Ministry of Sound ins Leben rief.

House 1. Le DJ et producteur de « house music » Paul Oakenfold, qui inaugura le super club Ministry of Sound de Londres au début des années 1990.

HAYLEY MADDEN/S.I.N.

House proud 2. Norman Cook, better known as Fatboy Slim, performing at the Glastonbury Festival, 1998. Cook was a proponent of the Big Beat sound. His remix of Cornershop's *Brimful of Asha* spent weeks at No. 1 in the British charts.

Bei uns zu House 2. Norman Cook, besser bekannt als Fatboy Slim, tritt beim 1998er Glastonbury Festival auf. Cook war einer der maßgeblichen Akteure, die den Big-Beat-Sound populär machten. Sein Remix des Cornershop-Stücks *Brimful of Asha* belegte wochenlang den ersten Platz der britischen Charts.

House 2. Norman Cook, plus connu sous le nom de Fatboy Slim, « joue » au Glastonbury Festival, en 1998. Cook fut l'un des créateurs du son Big Beat. Son remix de *Brimful of Asha* de Cornershop resta plusieurs semaines en tête des charts britanniques.

8. Fashion
Mode
La mode

As a preliminary to the World Cup, ready-to-wear fashion houses organised their own football match at the Stade de France, Paris, 25 May 1998. Here the midfield is dominated by a John Galliano creation.

Im Vorfeld der Fußballweltmeisterschaft organisierten Prêt-à-porter-Modehäuser ihr eigenes Fußballmatch im Pariser Stade de France, 25. Mai 1998. Hier wird das Mittelfeld von einer John-Galliano-Kreation dominiert.

Les maisons de haute couture et de prêt-à-porter avaient organisé leur propre match au Stade de France, à Paris, le 25 mai 1998, en préliminaire à la Coupe du monde de football. On voit ici le milieu de terrain occupé par une créature de John Galliano.

8. Fashion
Mode
La mode

There were beautiful clothes. There were designer clothes. And, in some cases, there were beautiful designer clothes. The Nineties were the age of the label – Armani, Gucci, Versace and dozens more. *Haute couture* came down from its lofty catwalks to reach 'off the peg' and everyday levels. Schoolchildren refused to wear school uniform unless its components came from Pierre Cardin and company. It was fashionable to be pencil slim. Supermodels such as Kate Moss and Naomi Campbell became richer and more famous than many a movie actress, but no one had more style than Diana, Princess of Wales.

Designs reflected the principles that governed the world of art. What mattered was shocking the beholder. Clothes became outrageously ugly, brilliantly bizarre, eye-catchingly eccentric in colour, material and shape. Such design, in turn, provoked a counter-fashion for a return to more folksy, homespun designs and materials.

And there were the customary revivals... of the Forties, the Fifties, the Sixties. Those in the know quietly put their Nineties clothes away, aware that the 'shock of the new' would one day become fashionably retro.

In den neunziger Jahren gab es schöne Kleidung. Es gab Designerkleidung. Und – manchmal – gab es schöne Designerkleidung. Es war ein Jahrzehnt der Labels – Armani, Gucci, Versace und Dutzende mehr. Die Haute Couture stieg von ihren erhabenen Laufstegen hinab und fand sich „auf der Stange" und im Alltag wieder. Schulkinder weigerten sich, ihre Schuluniform zu tragen, sofern sie nicht von Pierre Cardin kam.

Wer mit der Mode ging, musste spindeldürr sein. Supermodels wie Kate Moss und Naomi Campbell wurden reicher und berühmter als so manche Filmschauspielerin, aber keine von ihnen hatte so viel Stil wie Prinzessin Diana.

Das Modedesign spiegelte die herrschenden Prinzipien der Kunstwelt wider: Es kam zuvorderst darauf an, den Betrachter zu schockieren. So wurden die Kleider himmelschreiend hässlich, auf brillante Art bizarr, auffallend exzentrisch hinsichtlich Farbgestaltung, Form und Material. Diese Mode wiederum provozierte eine Gegenbewegung, die sich auf volkstümlichere, handgemachte Designs und Materialien besann.

Daneben gab es die üblichen Revivals ... die Vierziger, Fünfziger und Sechziger kamen zurück. Die Trendsetter motteten ihre Kleidung aus den neunziger Jahren still und heimlich ein, wohl wissend, dass der „Schock des Neuen" von heute der modische Retro-Look von morgen sein wird.

Il y avait de beaux vêtements. Il y avait des vêtements de couturiers. Et il y avait parfois de beaux vêtements de couturier. Les années quatre-vingt-dix furent l'époque des marques – Armani, Gucci, Versace et des dizaines d'autres. La Haute Couture descendait de sa haute estrade pour se mettre au niveau du « prêt-à-porter » et du quotidien. Et les écoliers refusaient de porter l'uniforme à moins qu'il ne soit dessiné par Pierre Cardin et compagnie.

Il était à la mode d'être mince comme un fil. Des mannequins vedette comme Kate Moss et Naomi Campbell devenaient plus riches et plus célèbres que nombre d'actrices de cinéma, mais aucune d'entre elles n'avait autant de style que Diana, la princesse de Galles.

Les modèles reflétaient les principes qui gouvernaient le monde de l'art. Il fallait choquer les spectateurs. Les vêtements devenaient outrageusement laids, brillamment bizarres, excentriques par leurs couleurs, leurs matières et leurs formes tape-à-l'œil. Et cette mode provoquait à son tour un mouvement contraire où l'on revenait à des matières plus populaires et à des coupes faites à la maison.

Et il y eut les habituels mouvement rétro… les années quarante, cinquante, soixante. Ceux qui s'habillaient encore simplement à la mode d'aujourd'hui rangèrent soigneusement au vestiaire leurs vêtements des années 1990, sûrs que ces « nouveautés choquantes » allaient un jour aussi redevenir à la mode.

The little girl look
beloved of pop stars
and 'men of a certain
age'. Kerry at
Submission, 1998.

Der Kleine-
Mädchen-Look
feierte große Erfolge
bei Popstars und
Männern im
fortgeschrittenen
Alter. Kerry im
Submission, 1998.

Le look Lolita, chéri
des pop stars et des
« hommes d'un
certain âge ». Kerry
au Submission,
en 1998.

Hiding behind their masks, revellers dance tongue-to-tongue at the Skin 2 Ball, London, December 1995.

Versteckt hinter ihren Masken tanzen diese Nachtschwärmer Zunge an Zunge beim Skin-2-Ball, London, Dezember 1995.

Dissimulés derrière leur masque, des clubbers dansent langue contre langue au Skin 2 Ball de Londres, en décembre 1995.

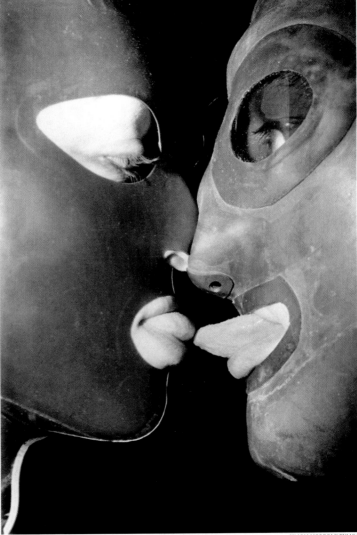

SIMON NORFOLK/PYMCA

In happier days, Liz Hurley and Hugh Grant arrive at the FWAF party, London, 11 May 1994. (Dress and safety pins by Versace.)

In glücklicheren Tagen: Liz Hurleys und Hugh Grants Ankunft auf der FWAF Party in London, 11. Mai 1994 (Kleid und Sicherheitsnadeln von Versace).

Aux temps heureux, Liz Hurley (robe et épingles de sûreté de Versace) et Hugh Grant arrivent à la soirée du FWAF, organisée à Londres le 11 mai 1994.

MAURO CARRARO/COLORIFIC!

Julia Roberts arrives at the premiere of *Notting Hill*, London, 27 April 1999. Some delicate souls were upset by her armpits.

Julia Roberts bei der Premiere des Films *Notting Hill*, London, 27. April 1999. Zartere Gemüter empfanden ihre unrasierten Achseln als Affront.

Julia Roberts vient assister à la première de *Coup de foudre à Notting Hill*, à Londres le 27 avril 1999. Certaines âmes sensibles furent scandalisées par ses aisselles.

IAN WALDIE/REUTERS/ARCHIVE PHOTOS

Kate Moss relaxes in a ready-to-wear dress at the Thierry Mugler autumn/winter show, Paris, March 1995.

Kate Moss entspannt sich in einem Prêt-à-porter-Kleid bei der Präsentation von Thierry Muglers Herbst-Winter-Kollektion, Paris, März 1995.

Kate Moss fait une pause dans une robe de la collection de prêt-à-porter automne-hiver de Thierry Mugler, à Paris, en mars 1995.

Christy Turlington (in curlers) and Naomi Campbell (reading) at the Oscar de la Renta autumn/winter show, New York City, 1993.

Christy Turlington (mit Lockenwicklern) und Naomi Campbell (mit Lektüre) bei Oscar de la Rentas Herbst-Winter-Schau, New York City, 1993.

Christy Turlington (en bigoudis) et Naomi Campbell (lisant) au défilé de la collection automne-hiver de Oscar de la Renta, à New York en 1993.

CHABASSIER/MPA/LIAISON AGENCY

The master of the bias-cut slip dress, John Galliano, with two of his models. The dresses were part of Galliano's autumn 1999 collection and exemplified his love of simplicity of design with subtle detailing.

John Galliano, Meister des schrägen Schnitts, mit zwei seiner Models. Die Kleider aus Gallianos 1999er Herbstkollektion verdeutlichen seine Liebe zu reduzierten Schnitten und subtilen Details.

Le maître du biaisé, John Galliano, avec deux de ses mannequins. Ces robes, qui faisaient partie de la collection Automne 1999 de Galliano, sont exemplaires de l'amour de la coupe simple et des détails subtils du couturier.

The Stars and
Stripes are put to
fashionable use in
another Galliano
dress, from his 1993
summer collection.

Stars and Stripes im
Dienste der Mode:
ein weiteres
Galliano-Kleid aus
der Sommerkollek-
tion des Jahres
1993.

Une autre robe de
Galliano, apparte-
nant à sa collection
Été 1993, taillée
dans le drapeau
américain.

Jean Paul Gaultier goes down on one knee before his own creation for the spring/summer collection of 1996, Paris.

Jean Paul Gaultier geht vor seiner eigenen Schöpfung für die Frühjahr-Sommer-Kollektion 1996 in die Knie, Paris.

Jean Paul Gaultier à genoux devant une de ses créations pour la collection Printemps-Été 1996, à Paris.

Alexander McQueen, however, appears to have doubts about a dress he designed for the same collection.

Alexander McQueen dagegen scheint Zweifel an seinem Entwurf für dieselbe Kollektion zu haben.

Alexander McQueen paraît douter de la robe qu'il a dessinée pour la même collection.

J J CECCARINI/COLORIFIC!

Pop goes the fashion. Ginger Spice (Geri Halliwell) sports a size 6 Union Jack at the 1997 Brit Awards.

Pop goes Fashion. Ginger Spice (Geri Halliwell) trägt bei den 1997er Brit Awards einen Union Jack in Größe 34.

Mode pop. Ginger Spice (Geri Halliwell), simplement couverte du drapeau de la Grande-Bretagne, taille 34, lors des Brit Awards 1997.

KIERAN DOHERTY/REUTERS/ARCHIVE PHOTOS

Madonna revels in a typical Jean Paul Gaultier corset-fronted outfit on her Blonde Ambition Tour, 1990.

Madonna schwelgt in einem typischen Jean-Paul-Gaultier-Outfit im Korsett-Stil während ihrer Blonde-Ambition-Tour, 1990.

Madonna dans le corset à bonnets pointus que lui a dessiné Jean Paul Gaultier pour son Blonde Ambition Tour de 1990.

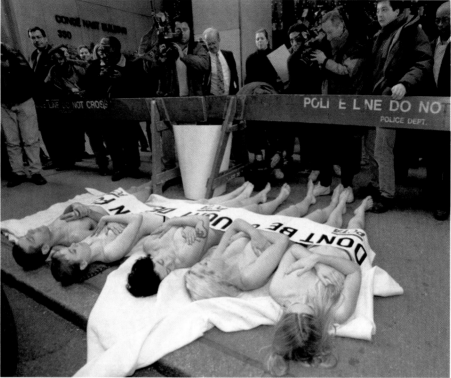

JEFF CHRISTENSEN/REUTERS/ARCHIVE PHOTOS

Members of the People for the Ethical Treatment of Animals protest group stage a naked protest outside the offices of American *Vogue*, New York City, 17 December 1997. They objected to the magazine's promotion of fur coats.

Mitglieder einer Tierschutzvereinigung protestieren nackt vor den Büroräumen der amerikanischen *Vogue* gegen die Befürwortung von Pelzmänteln durch das Magazin, New York City, 17. Dezember 1997.

Des membres du groupe People for the Ethical Treatment of Animals manifestent nus devant les bureaux de *Vogue* Amérique, à New York, le 17 décembre 1997. Ils protestaient contre la publicité faite par le magazine aux vêtements de fourrure.

Modelling a protest
skirt at Sonja
Nuttall's show,
London, 12 March
1995. The slogan
reads 'Put smoking
out of fashion'.

Laufstegprotest bei
einer Modenschau
von Sonja Nuttall
in London,
12. März 1995.
Der Slogan auf
dem Rock: „Bringt
das Rauchen aus
der Mode."

Une jupe protesta-
taire présentée lors
du défilé de la collec-
tion Sonja Nuttall,
le 12 mars 1995.
Le slogan dit :
« Sortez le tabagisme
de la mode ».

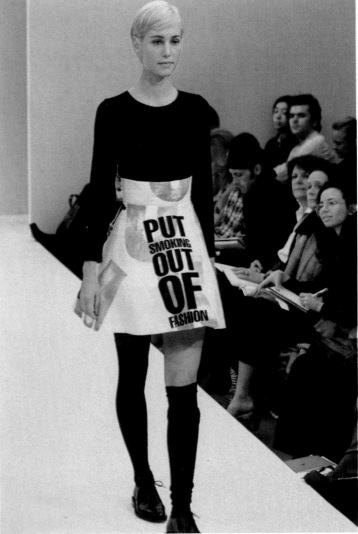

PA

Supermodel goes second-hand. Naomi
Campbell examines the delights of
Portobello Market, London.

Ein Supermodel kauft aus zweiter Hand.
Naomi Campbell erfreut sich am Angebot des
Londoner Portobello Market.

Un mannequin aux puces. Naomi Campbell
admire les trésors du marché de Portobello,
à Londres.

'There goes my gun.' Tupak Shakur displays the season's must-have accessory in his short-lived gangsta rap career, 1993.

„Hier steckt meine Knarre." Tupak Shakur posiert mit dem ultimativen Accessoire der Saison während seiner kurzlebigen Gangsta-Rap-Karriere, 1993.

« La place de mon canon ». Tupak Shakur expose en 1993 l'accessoire obligé du gangsta raper qu'il fut brièvement.

Snoop Doggy Dogg
holds up his Dogg
Pound Gang jacket
at the *Billboard*
Music Awards,
Los Angeles, 1994.

Snoop Doggy Dogg
hält bei den Bill-
board Music Awards
seine Dogg Pound
Gang-Jacke in die
Höhe, Los Angeles,
1994.

Snoop Doggy Dogg
montre sa veste
brodée au nom du
Dogg Pound Gang
lors du Billboard
Music Awards à Los
Angeles, en 1994.

ROB WATKINS/PYMCA

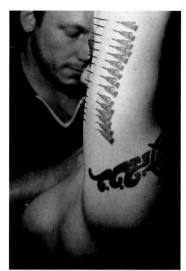

JAY BROOKS/PYMCA

JAMES LANGE/PYMCA

ROB WATKINS/PYMCA

(Clockwise from top left) Ear piercing; syringe piercing; a combat skirt of 1998; and Black Hair and Beauty at Alexandra Palace, London, 1999.

(Im Uhrzeigersinn, von oben links) Ohrenpiercing; Spritzenpiercing; ein Kampfrock aus dem Jahre 1998; schwarze Haare, schwarze Schönheit im Londoner Alexandra Palace, 1999.

(Dans le sens des aiguilles d'une montre) Piercing à l'oreille ; piercing d'aiguilles ; jupe de combat de 1998 ; et Black Hair and Beauty à l'Alexandra Palace de Londres en 1999.

Take a hike…
Michiko Koshino
models a fashionable
front strap rucksack,
1999.

Lass uns wandern
gehen … Michiko
Koshino präsentiert
einen modischen
Ein-Gurt-Rucksack,
der auf den
Bauch geschnallt
wird, 1999.

Pour la promenade…
Le mannequin
Michiko Koshino
présente un sac à
dos frontal à la
mode, en 1999.

PA

Bare-cheeked face:
scenes from a
clubber's life.
A rave, somewhere
in Ibiza, 1999.

Wange an Wange:
Szenen aus dem
Clubleben, hier
bei einem Rave
irgendwo auf
Ibiza, 1999.

Scènes de la vie de
clubber. De bonnes
joues fraîches pour
une rave, quelque
part à Ibiza en 1999.

JAY BROOKS/PYMCA

Standing up and cooling off. Designer gear, designer mineral water in Hoxton Square, London, 1994.

Aufstehen und abkühlen. Designer-klamotten und Designermineral-wasser im Hoxton Square. London, 1994.

Afficher sa marque. Des fringues de designer et une eau minérale de designer à Hoxton Square, à Londres, en 1994.

LIZ JOHNSON ARTUR/PYMCA

9. Youth
Jugend
La jeunesse

'...and would you like that gift-wrapped?' A shop that positively
bulged with something for the weekend – one of the Ann Summers
sex shops, Cardiff, Wales, 1998.

„... soll ich es Ihnen als Geschenk einpacken?" In diesem Laden –
einer von Ann Summers' Sexshops in Cardiff, Wales – gibt es alles für
ein im besten Sinne abgerundetes Wochenende, 1998.

« ... désirez-vous un paquet cadeau ? » Cette boutique est littéralement
remplie de choses utiles pour le week-end – l'un des sex-shops de Ann
Summers, à Cardiff (Pays de Galles), en 1998.

9. Youth
Jugend
La jeunesse

To be young, with a job, friends, money in your pocket and a sense of purpose in life, the Nineties were a great time to be alive. Ageing populations needed youth to prime the economic pump and to inject energy and momentum into everyday living. The shops were full of the good things in life… clothes and footwear, discs, bikes, sugar-sweet alcoholic drinks, fast food, and all the trappings of that blissful entry into adult life.

To have no job meant to have no money, no power, no style, no hope. The streets of most major cities still provided a hard, cold bed for an increasing number of young people. Drugs provided desperate and momentary relief. The passing crowds provided an unceasing reminder of what could be.

But, for the lucky, life partied on. There were clubs, bars, raves, brawls, nights on the town, lads on the pull, girls on the loose. And there were plenty of role models to inspire young people with the will to succeed, to make a fortune, reach the top, snatch at fame.

Für die Jugend waren die neunziger Jahre eine großartige Zeit, vorausgesetzt, man hatte einen Job, Freunde, Geld in der Tasche und ein Lebensziel vor Augen. Die im Durchschnitt immer ältere Bevölkerung brauchte die Jugend, um die Wirtschaft anzukurbeln und neuen Schwung und Energie in den Alltag zu bringen. Die Geschäfte waren voll von den guten Dingen des Lebens … Kleidung und Schuhe, Platten, Bikes, zuckersüße Spirituosen, Fast Food und all den anderen Verlockungen des segensreichen Übergangs in das Erwachsenenleben.

Wer keinen Job hatte, hatte kein Geld, keine Macht, keinen Stil, keine Hoffnung. Die Straßen der meisten Großstädte waren die harte, kalte Schlafstatt für eine wachsende Zahl junger Menschen. Drogen sorgten oft für bitter benötigte, wenn auch nur kurz währende Ablenkung. Und die vorbeiziehenden Menschenmassen waren eine ständige Erinnerung daran, wie das Leben hätte sein können.

Für die glücklicheren jedoch war das Leben eine endlose Party. Es gab Clubs, Bars, Raves, Gegröle, Nächte in der Stadt, attraktive Jungs und enthemmte Mädchen. Dazu gab es genügend Vorbilder, denen junge Leute mit dem Willen, erfolgreich zu sein, Geld zu machen, an die Spitze zu kommen und berühmt zu werden, nacheifern konnten.

Pour un jeune avec un travail, des amis, de l'argent en poche et la conscience de l'utilité de la vie, les années 1990 furent une grande époque. Les populations vieillissantes avaient besoin de la jeunesse pour réamorcer la pompe économique et injecter de l'énergie et du dynamisme dans la vie quotidienne. Les boutiques étaient pleines de bonnes choses … vêtements et chaussures, disques, bicyclettes, boissons alcoolisées sucrées, fast-foods et tous ces signes extérieurs marquant l'entrée dans une vie adulte merveilleuse.

Ne pas avoir de travail impliquait n'avoir ni argent, ni pouvoir, ni élégance, ni espoir. Les rues de la plupart des grandes villes offraient toujours une couche dure et froide à un nombre croissant de jeunes. La drogue leur était un soulagement momentané et désespéré. La foule des passants leur rappelait sans cesse ce qu'ils auraient pu être.

Mais, pour les plus chanceux, la vie n'était que plaisirs. Il y avait des clubs, des bars, des raves, des rixes, des sorties en ville, des garçons en drague, des filles libérées. Et il y existait d'innombrables modèles capables d'inspirer des jeunes désireux de réussir, de faire fortune, d'atteindre les sommets et d'acquérir la célébrité.

A commonplace scene: …skinning up, London 1994. Television and drugs offered escape from the harsh realities of life for a great many young people in the 1990s.

Eine weit verbreitete Szenerie: In einem Londoner Wohnzimmer wird ein Joint gedreht. Das Fernsehen und Drogen boten für viele junge Menschen in den neunziger Jahren eine willkommene Abwechslung von der harten Lebenswirklichkeit, 1994.

Un décor ordinaire : … le petit joint du matin, à Londres en 1994. La télévision et la drogue permirent à beaucoup de jeunes des années 1990 de s'évader de la dure réalité du quotidien.

TYRONE TURNER/BLACK STAR/COLORIFIC!

Members of a teenage gang 'Dangerous Bones' check their weapons. Most such gangs were mutual protection societies against a world that young people saw as unnervingly dangerous.

Mitglieder der Teenagergang „Dangerous Bones" überprüfen ihre Waffen. Die meisten dieser Gangs waren Schutzgemeinschaften auf Gegenseitigkeit vor einer Welt, die von vielen Jugendlichen als feindselig und gefährlich empfunden wurde.

Des membres d'un gang d'adolescents, les « Dangerous Bones », vérifient leurs armes. La plupart de ces gangs constituaient des sociétés de protection mutuelle contre un monde que les jeunes voyaient comme dangereusement déconcertant.

CHERYL HIMMELSTEIN/BLACK STAR/COLORIFIC!

The fruits of further education. Two teenage mothers in high school graduation day mortarboards and gowns pose with their infant children. Much of the stigma attaching to teenage pregnancy had been lifted, but the burden remained.

Die Früchte höherer Bildung. Zwei jugendliche Mütter im Absolventendress posieren mit ihren Kindern bei der Abschlussfeier. Obwohl die Stigmatisierung von Müttern im Teenager-Alter zurückgegangen ist, blieb die Bürde erhalten.

Les fruits de l'éducation. Deux jeunes mères en robe et mortier de fin d'études posent avec leur enfant. Même si on n'accablait plus les adolescentes enceintes, elles devaient néanmoins en supporter le fardeau.

JOSEF POLLEROSS/ANZENBERGER/COLORIFIC!

(Above and opposite) Locked up on both sides of the world. (Above) Inmates at a prison colony for 16- to 18-year-olds, Mariinsk, Russia, 1992. For the most part, their crimes consisted of rape, robbery or murder.

(Oben und gegenüberliegende Seite) Eingesperrt an beiden Enden der Welt. (Oben) Häftlinge einer Gefängniskolonie für 16- bis 18-jährige Straftäter im russischen Mariinsk, 1992. Zum größten Teil setzten sich ihre Verbrechen aus Vergewaltigung, Raub und Mord zusammen.

(Ci-dessus et ci-contre) Enfermés de part et d'autre du monde. (Ci-dessus) Des prisonniers dans une colonie pénitentiaire pour les 16–18 ans, à Mariinsk (Russie), en 1992, pour la plupart condamnés pour viol, vol ou meurtre.

MIKE FIALA/LIAISON AGENCY

Canvas prison. (Above) Some of the 1,400 young detainees at the Maricopa County 'Pup Tent City', Phoenix, Arizona, 23 December 1998. Tent cities were set up to ease the overcrowding of conventional prisons.

Gefangen im Zelt. (Oben) Einige der 1400 jungen Delinquenten in der „Pup Tent City" von Maricopa County in Phoenix, Arizona, 23. Dezember 1998. Solche Zeltstädte wurden errichtet, um die Überfüllung herkömmlicher Strafanstalten zu mildern.

Prison de toile. (Ci-dessus) Une partie des 1 400 jeunes détenus sous la « Pup Tent City » du Maricopa County, à Phoenix (Arizona), le 23 décembre 1998. Ces villages de tentes étaient érigés pour soulager la surpopulation des prisons conventionnelles.

ERICA LANSNER/BLACK STAR/COLORIFIC!

Twenty-five years on from the original rock festival at Woodstock, an attempt was made to revive the spirit and freedom of those three days of peace, love and music in 1969. Even with the obligatory substances (above), the 1994 festival failed miserably.

25 Jahre nach dem ursprünglichen Woodstock-Festival wurde der Versuch unternommen, den Geist der Freiheit von drei Tagen Frieden, Liebe und Musik aus dem Jahre 1969 wieder zu beleben. Selbst die obligatorischen „Substanzen" spielten eine Rolle (siehe oben). Dennoch scheiterte das Festival von 1994 kläglich.

Vingt-cinq ans après le festival rock de Woodstock, il y eut une tentative pour faire revivre l'esprit et la liberté de ces trois jours de paix, d'amour et de musique de 1969. Mais ce festival fut un échec retentissant malgré la consommation quasi obligatoire de certaines substances (ci-dessus).

RICHARD BELAND/S.I.N.

The rain and the mud were still there, but that essential hippie culture of the late 1960s had long ago been buried under the new materialism of the late 20th century.

Obwohl Matsch und Regen immer noch da waren, war die Essenz der Hippiekultur der späten sechziger Jahre längst unter dem neuen Materialismus des ausgehenden 20. Jahrhunderts begraben.

La pluie et la boue étaient là mais la culture hippie qui était l'essence de la fin des années 1960 avait été depuis longtemps effacée par le nouveau matérialisme de la fin du XXᵉ siècle.

RICK FRIEDMAN/BLACK STAR/COLORIFIC!

The spirit was willing, the flesh was willing, but such events as the
Rainbow Gathering at Vermont in 1991 (above) were merely brief
escapes from the routine of comfortable and well-ordered life.

Der Geist war willig, das Fleisch war willig, doch Veranstaltungen wie das
Rainbow Gathering in Vermont im Jahre 1991 (oben) waren nicht mehr
als kurze Ausflüchte aus einem komfortablen, wohl geordneten Leben.

L'esprit le désirait, la chair le voulait, mais des événements comme le
Rainbow Gathering à Vermont en 1991 (ci-dessus) tenaient plus de l'envie
de quitter brièvement la routine d'une vie confortable et bien ordonnée
que d'une véritable aspiration à la liberté sociale.

Nature spoils what
might have been a
great gig. A fan
arises from the slime
of the Glastonbury
Festival, Somerset,
1997.

Die Natur macht
einem potenziell
großen Auftritt
einen Strich durch
die Rechnung. Ein
Fan erhebt sich beim
1997er Glastonbury
Festival im engli-
schen Somerset aus
dem Schlamm.

Les caprices de la
nature ont malheu-
reusement gâché le
Glastonbury Festival,
organisé dans le
Somerset en 1997 et
qui aurait pu être un
grand concert. Une
fan se délectant dans
la boue.

MELANIE COX/S.I.N.

DAVID SWINDELLS/PYMCA

It's a club, an empire, and a way of life. Travis the Bongo drives
regulars to steam and sweat their way through an evening at
'Twice As Nice', a British garage night started in 1996.

Ein Club, ein Königreich, ein Lebensstil. Der Musiker Travis the
Bongo setzt das Stammpublikum der 1996 in Großbritannien ins
Leben gerufenen „Twice as Nice"-Veranstaltungsreihe unter
Dampf und Schweiß.

C'est un club, un empire et un mode de vie. Travis, le joueur de
bongo, chauffe les habitués de la « Twice As Nice », une soirée
UK garage lancée en 1996.

MATT SMITH/PYMCA

Out of it but still there. 'Infamous' might at Lakota, Bristol, early 1990s. Ecstacy, trip hop, Tricky and Portishead were all part of the Bristol scene at the time.

Nur noch körperlich anwesend. Die „Infamous"-Clubnacht im Lakota, Bristol, Anfang 1990. Die Droge Ecstacy, Trip Hop sowie die Bands Tricky und Portishead waren allesamt Teil der Bristoler Szene zu jener Zeit.

En marge mais in. Nuit « Infâme » à Lakota (Bristol) au début des années 1990. Ecstasy, trip hop, Tricky et Portishead faisaient alors partie de la scène de Bristol.

DARREN REGMER/PYMCA

Plenty of fun, but with strings attached, at the Torture Garden,
London, 1998. The dividing line between pain and pleasure became
hopelessly blurred for many in the 1990s.

Spaß an der Leine im Londoner Torture Garden, 1998. Für manche
verschwamm die Grenze zwischen Schmerz und Lust in den neunziger
Jahren auf hoffnungslose Art und Weise.

Beaucoup de plaisir sans doute mais liés seulement par des cordelettes,
au Torture Garden de Londres, en 1998. La frontière entre douleur et
plaisir a été complètement effacée pendant une grande partie des
années 1990.

JAY BROOKS/PYMCA

The taste of true freedom in the glorious years that followed the collapse of Communism in Czechoslovakia for two revellers in a Prague club, 1998. How different from the old Party life.

Den Geschmack der wahren Freiheit in den glorreichen Tagen nach dem Zusammenbruch des Kommunismus in Tschechien genießen diese beiden Nachtschwärmer in einem Prager Club, 1998. Das Party-Leben unterscheidet sich halt deutlich vom Partei-Leben.

Deux gays d'un club de Prague goûtent à la vraie liberté, quelques années après l'effondrement du communisme en Tchécoslovaquie en 1998. Une ambiance très différente de la vie quotidienne sous l'ancien parti.

DEREK RIDGERS/PYMCA

Club or concert, it didn't matter. There was always the chance
that someone would be overcome by the music, the ambience,
the booze… as in this scene in Albuquerque, New Mexico, 1990.

Club oder Konzert, was macht das für einen Unterschied? Die
Wahrscheinlichkeit war immer groß, dass jemand von der Musik,
der Atmosphäre, dem Alkohol überwältigt wurde … in diesem Fall
in Albuquerque, New Mexico, 1990.

Club ou concert, peu importe. Il subsiste toujours le risque que
quelqu'un se laisse emporter par la musique, l'ambiance, la boisson…
comme ici à Albuquerque (Nouveau Mexique) en 1990.

Someone gimme a break: the Wag, one of London's top dance clubs, 1997.

Gib mir einen Break: The Wag, einer von Londons großen Dance-Clubs, 1997.

L'occasion de se faire remarquer au Wag, un des grands clubs de danse de Londres, en 1997.

JAY BROOKS/PYMCA

HENRY IDDON/PYMCA

Away from the club scene there was plenty of fresh air and fun for those with more bravery than sense of self-preservation. (Above) Free-riding on the snowy slopes of La Clusaz, France, 1998.

Weitab der Clubszene gab es genügend frische Luft und Fun für diejenigen, die über mehr Mut als Selbsterhaltungstrieb verfügten. (Oben) Freestyle-Snowboarding auf den winterlichen Hängen von La Clusaz, Frankreich, 1998.

Loin des clubs, ceux qui avaient plus de courage physique que de sens du risque retrouvaient l'air pur et le plaisir pur de l'effort. (Ci-dessus) Free-ride sur les pentes neigeuses de La Clusaz (France), en 1998.

ELIO LOCCISANO/ANZENBERGER/COLORIFIC!

With not a moment's thought for the consequences of the line
breaking or the strain on his spine, a base jumper takes off from the
heights overlooking Sydney Harbour, Australia.

Ohne auch nur einen Moment über die Folgen eines gerissenen Seils
oder einer gebrochenen Wirbelsäule nachzudenken, stürzt sich dieser
Bungee-Jumper aus höchster Höhe über dem Hafen von Sydney,
Australien, in die Tiefe.

Sans penser aux conséquences d'une rupture de l'élastique ou des
efforts subis par sa colonne vertébrale, ce sauteur s'envole depuis les
hauteurs dominant le port de Sydney, en Australie.

ANDY HALL

Was it all worthwhile? The day of reckoning as sixth-form
students get their A-level exam results, Chenderit School,
19 August 1999.

War es das wert? Der Tag der Abrechnung für diese Schul-
abgänger bei der Entgegennahme ihrer Abschlusszeugnisse,
Chenderit School, Großbritannien, 19. August 1999.

Tout cela en valait-il la peine ? Le jour du Jugement : des
élèves de terminale de la Chenderit School reçoivent leurs
résultats du baccalauréat, le 19 août 1999.

MURDO MACLEOD

And will it all be worthwhile? Freshers (first-year students) enjoy ritual humiliation in the traditionally lukewarm welcome to university by second-year students, St Andrews, Scotland.

Und wird es das wert sein? Erstsemester genießen ihre rituelle Demütigung beim traditionell feucht-fröhlichen Empfang durch die höheren Semester der schottischen St.-Andrews-Universität.

Et cela en vaudra-t-il la peine ? Accueil à l'université : les étudiants de première année subissent l'épreuve traditionnelle du bizutage que leur infligent les étudiants de seconde année de St Andrews (Écosse).

DAVID TURNLEY/BLACK STAR/COLORIFIC!

(Above and opposite) Punks and monks, a story of contrasting though related philosophies. (Above) A break in the customary meditation for Tibetan Buddhist monks at the Dharamsala Monastery, India, January 1999.

(Oben und gegenüberliegende Seite) Punks und Mönche, eine Geschichte ganz unterschiedlicher und doch verwandter Philosophien. (Oben) Tibetische Mönche des Dharamsala-Klosters während einer Meditationspause, Indien, Januar 1999.

(Ci-dessus et ci-contre) Punks et moines, deux philosophies opposées et proches. (Ci-dessus) Petite pause entre deux méditations pour des moines bouddhistes tibétains du monastère de Dharamsala (Inde), en janvier 1999.

An alternative way of freeing oneself from the restrictions and routines of society. Punks on a New York City street, 1996. Though not as old as Buddhism, the Punk movement was into its third generation.

Ein anderer Weg, sich von den Beschränkungen und der Routine der Gesellschaft loszulösen. Punks in den Straßen von New York City, 1996. Obwohl nicht ganz so alt wie der Buddhismus, ging die Punk-Bewegung bereits in die dritte Generation.

Un autre moyen de se libérer des interdits et de la routine. Des punks dans une rue de New York, en 1996. Bien qu'il ne soit pas aussi ancien que le bouddhisme, le mouvement punk en est déjà à sa troisième génération.

10. Sport
Sport
Le sport

Ronaldo cuts a swathe through the Moroccan defence as Brazil win their Group A match 3-0 during the World Cup preliminaries in Nantes, France, 16 June 1998.

Ronaldo spielt die marokkanische Abwehr schwindelig. Brasilien gewann das Weltmeisterschafts-Vorrundenspiel der Gruppe A gegen Marokko mit 3:0 in Nantes, Frankreich, 16. Juni 1998.

Ronaldo transperce la défense du Maroc lors du match préliminaire du Groupe A à l'occasion de la Coupe du monde à Nantes, le 16 juin 1998, qui voit le Brésil gagner par 3 à 0.

10. Sport
Sport
Le sport

Never before had so much time, money and newsprint been devoted to sport. The private lives of footballers, athletes, tennis players, boxers, Grand Prix drivers and even match-fixing cricketers were minutely examined and posted for all to see. The cult of sporting celebrity ensured that all play and no work made Jack a very rich boy.

Basketball, ice hockey, baseball and golf increased their international appeal – thanks largely to coverage by television channels which had lost out in the auctions of rights to televise the more popular sports. The Olympic Games passed by happily enough in Barcelona in 1992, but in Atlanta in 1996 they were marred by a terrorist bomb that killed two and injured well over a hundred.

Football became the greatest sporting money-spinner of all time, with a proliferation of international and continental tournaments. Players' salaries reached ludicrous levels. Managers walked a weekly tightrope, their jobs secure only while the team performed well. And it cost fans dear to watch the game they loved and to wear replica strips manufactured in the Third World.

Niemals zuvor wurde so viel Zeit, Geld und Zeitungspapier dem Sport gewidmet. Das Privatleben von Fußballern, Leichtathleten, Tennisspielern, Boxern, Formel-1-Fahrern und sogar Kricketspielern wurde minutiös durchleuchtet und öffentlich gemacht. Der Kult um die Sport treibenden Berühmtheiten sorgte für massiven Reichtum aufseiten der Aktiven.

Basketball, Eishockey, Baseball und Golf konnten weltweit ihren Ruf aufwerten – nicht zuletzt dank der Berichterstattung derjenigen TV-Sender, die beim Bieten um Übertragungs-rechte an populäreren Sportarten den Kürzeren gezogen hatten. Die Olympischen Spiele 1992 in Barcelona gingen reibungslos über die Bühne, während die Spiele vier Jahre später in Atlanta von einem Bombenanschlag überschattet wurden, der zwei Todesopfer und über 100 Verletzte forderte.

Fußball wurde zum größten Geld-Umschlagplatz in der Geschichte des Sports, einhergehend mit einer Zunahme von internationalen und kontinentalen Turnieren. Die Gehälter der Spieler schossen in astronomische Höhen, während Trainer einen wöchentlichen Drahtseilakt vollführen mussten – schließlich war ihr Job nur so lange sicher, wie ihr Team gut spielte. Die Fans mussten derweil tief in die Tasche greifen, um ihre Lieblingsmannschaft zu sehen und in der Dritten Welt gefertigte Trikots ihrer Stars zu tragen.

Jamais on n'avait consacré autant de temps, d'argent et de papier au sport. La vie privée des footballeurs, des athlètes, des joueurs de tennis, des boxeurs, des pilotes de Grand Prix – voire celle des joueurs de cricket – a été minutieusement observée et publiée dans tous ses détails. Le culte des vedettes du sport donnait l'impression que jouer sans travailler pouvait faire de quiconque un homme riche.

Le basket-ball, le hockey sur glace, le base-ball et le golf augmentaient leur audience internationale, en grande partie parce qu'ils pouvaient être couverts par les chaînes de télévision ayant perdu les enchères pour l'attribution des droits de retransmission des sports les plus populaires. Les Jeux olympiques se passèrent de manière assez heureuse à Barcelone en 1992 mais furent attristés à Atlanta en 1996 par une bombe terroriste qui tua deux personnes et en blessa plus d'une centaine.

Le football devenait la plus grosse mine d'or de tous les temps, grâce à la prolifération des tournois nationaux et internationaux. Les salaires des joueurs atteignaient des niveaux indécents. Les entraîneurs, dont le maintien ne dépendait plus que des résultats de leur équipe, avançaient chaque semaine sur la corde raide. Et les passionnés dépensaient beaucoup d'argent pour assister aux matches et porter les maillots de leurs joueurs favoris, fabriqués à bas prix dans le tiers-monde.

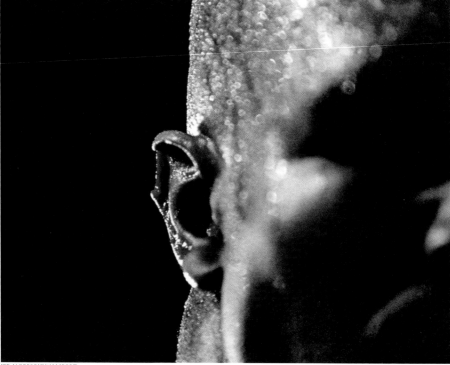

JED JACOBSOHN/ALLSPORT

The remains of Evander Holyfield's right ear after eleven rounds with Mike Tyson for the WBA Heavyweight title at the MGM Grand Garden, Las Vegas, 28 June 1997. Holyfield was not expected to win.

Was von Evander Holyfields rechtem Ohr nach 11 Runden Boxen gegen Mike Tyson um den WBA-Schwergewichtstitel übrig blieb. Der Kampf fand am 28. Juni 1997 im MGM Grand Garden von Las Vegas statt. Holyfield galt im Vorfeld als Außenseiter.

L'oreille droite d'Evander Holyfield mordue par Mike Tyson à la 11ᵉ reprise lors du combat pour le titre de champion du monde WBA des poids lourds, organisé à Las Vegas, le 28 juin 1997. Holyfield ne partait pas favori.

COLORIFIC!

The 1990s were not propitious for Tyson. In 1992 he was sentenced to six years in gaol for the rape of a beauty contestant in an Indianapolis hotel room. Five years later he was back in the ring, but Holyfield (right) outpunched him.

Die neunziger Jahre waren Tysons Unglücksjahre. 1992 wurde er wegen Vergewaltigung einer Teilnehmerin eines Schönheitswettbewerbs in einem Hotelzimmer in Indianapolis zu sechs Jahren Haft verurteilt. Fünf Jahre darauf kehrte er in den Ring zurück, nur um von Holyfield (rechts) besiegt zu werden.

Les années 1990 ne furent pas favorables à Tyson. En 1992, il fut condamné à six ans de prison pour avoir violé une participante à un concours de beauté dans une chambre d'un hôtel d'Indianapolis. Cinq ans plus tard, il remontait sur un ring mais se faisait surclasser par Holyfield (à droite).

British Formula 1
racing driver
Damon Hill at
the Spanish Grand
Prix, Barcelona,
30 May 1999.

Der britische For-
mel-1-Pilot Damon
Hill beim Großen
Preis von Spanien
in Barcelona,
30. Mai 1999.

Le pilote britan-
nique de Formule 1
Damon Hill
lors du Grand
Prix d'Espagne
à Barcelone,
le 30 mai 1999.

MARK THOMPSON/ALLSPORT

MICHAEL COOPER/ALLSPORT

Germany's Michael Schumacher takes his Ferrari into the pits during the same race. Schumacher finished third, his arch rival Hill seventh. The race was won by Mika Hakkinen in a McLaren.

Michael Schumacher fährt beim selben Rennen in die Boxengasse ein. Schumacher wurde Dritter, sein Erzrivale Hill Siebter. Das Rennen gewann Mika Hakkinen in seinem McLaren.

L'Allemand Michael Schumacher rentre aux stands avec sa Ferrari lors de la même épreuve. Schumacher termina troisième et son grand rival Hill septième. La course fut remportée par Mika Hakkinen sur McLaren.

The tears of Gazza.
Paul Gascoigne's
heart-broken
response to a yellow
card during
England's defeat
by West Germany
in the 1990 World
Cup semi-final,
Turin, Italy…

Gazzas Tränen.
Paul Gascoignes ver-
zweifelte Reaktion
auf seine gelbe Karte
bei der Halbfinal-
Niederlage Englands
gegen Deutschland
während der 1990er
Fußball-WM in
Italien. Das Spiel
fand in Turin statt …

« Gazza » – Paul
Gascoigne – pleure
après avoir écopé
d'un carton jaune
lors du match de
demi-finale de la
Coupe du monde
1990 à Turin (Italie),
où l'Angleterre fut
battue par l'Alle-
magne de l'Ouest …

...and West Germany go on to win the World Cup. Jürgen Kohler lifts the FIFA World Trophy after their 1-0 victory over Argentina in the final at the Olympic Stadium, Rome, 8 July 1990.

... und der Sieger Deutschland gewann schließlich auch die Weltmeister-schaft. Jürgen Kohler reckt die FIFA-Trophäe nach dem 1:0-Finalsieg gegen Argentinien im römischen Olympiastadion in die Höhe, 8. Juli 1990.

... cette même équipe d'Allemagne de l'Ouest qui remportera la Coupe du monde. Jürgen Kohler brandit la Coupe de la FIFA après la victoire de son équipe par 1 à 0 sur l'Argentine lors de la finale au Stade olympique de Rome, le 8 juillet 1990.

Sheffield-born
Prince Naseem
Hamed executes a
jubilant backflip
after his first round
victory over Billy
Hardy, Manchester,
3 May 1997.

Der in Sheffield
geborene Prinz
Naseem Hamed
vollführt einen
Rückwärtssalto im
Jubel um seinen Sieg
gegen Billy Hardy
in der ersten Runde,
Manchester,
3. Mai 1997.

Le prince Naseem
Hamed, né à
Sheffield, exécute
un salto arrière dans
la joie d'avoir
remporté la victoire
au premier round
sur Billy Hardy,
à Manchester,
le 3 mai 1997.

SIMON BRUTY/ALLSPORT

Eye on the ball… Jana Novotna of Czechoslovakia at full stretch during the final of the women's singles at the Grand Slam Australian Open, 1991. In 1998 she won the women's singles at Wimbledon, beating Nathalie Tauziat 6-4, 7-6.

Den Ball im Auge … die Tschechin Jana Novotna streckt sich im Damen-Einzel-Finale der 1991er Australian Open nach dem Ball. 1998 bezwang sie im Endspiel des Damen-Einzels von Wimbledon Nathalie Tauziat mit 6:4 und 7:6.

L'œil sur la balle … La Tchécoslovaque Iana Novotna en pleine détente lors de la finale du simple dames de l'Open d'Australie en 1991. En 1998, elle remportait la finale de Wimbledon en battant Nathalie Tauziat 6-4, 7-6.

Knees on the
grass… Richard
Krajicek breaks
the Sampras run,
Wimbledon,
7 July 1996.

Die Knie im Gras …
Richard Krajicek
durchbricht die
Siegesserie von
Sampras, Wimble-
don, 7. Juli 1996.

À genoux dans
l'herbe … Richard
Krajicek brise
l'élan de Sampras
à Wimbledon,
le 7 juillet 1996.

Choisty clears
Becher's Brook in
the 1998 Grand
National, Aintree,
Liverpool. Two
years later Choisty
won a virtual
reality National
on a computer.

Das Militarypferd
Choisty überspringt
die Hürde Becher's
Brook beim 1998er
Grand National in
Aintree, Liverpool.
Zwei Jahre später
gewann Choisty ein
virtuelles National
am Computer.

Choisty franchit le
Becher's Brook,
célèbre obstacle du
Grand National
d'Aintree, près de
Liverpool. Deux
ans plus tôt, Choisty
remportait le
National mais en
mode virtuel sur
un ordinateur.

Battle of the giants. Magic Johnson of the LA Lakers (left) watches as Michael Jordan (Chicago Bulls) puts more points on the board.

Kampf der Giganten. Magic Johnson von den LA Lakers (links) schaut zu, wie Michael Jordan (Chicago Bulls) punktet.

Une bataille de géants. Impuissant, Magic Johnson, des LA Lakers (à gauche) regarde Michael Jordan (des Chicago Bulls) marquer un panier.

RICK STEWART/ALLSPORT

New kid on the block. Vince Carter of the Raptors leaps for glory at the NBA All-Star Slam Dunk contest, Oakland, California.

New Kid on the Block. Vince Carter von den Raptors springt beim NBA-All-Star-Slam-Dunk-Wettbewerb zum Ruhm, Oakland, Kalifornien.

Des nouveaux sur le parquet. Vince Carter, des Raptors, bondit pour la gagne lors du match All-Star Slam Dunk de la NBA, disputé à Oakland (Californie).

JED JACOBSOHN/ALLSPORT

GARY M PRIOR/ALLSPORT

Pete Sampras plants a winner's kiss on the men's singles trophy after his victory over Goran Ivanisevic, 6-7, 7-6, 6-4, 3-6, 6-2, in the final at Wimbledon, July 1998. It was his fifth Wimbledon title.

Pete Sampras' Kuss auf den Siegerpokal nach seinem Finalsieg im Herren-Einzel von Wimbledon über Goran Ivanisevic. Das Endspiel im 1998er Wimbledon-Turnier gewann Sampras mit 6:7, 7:6, 6:4, 3:6 und 6:2 – sein fünfter Wimbledon-Titel.

Pete Sampras embrasse la coupe du simple messieurs après sa victoire sur Goran Ivanisevic (6-7, 7-6, 6-4, 3-6, 6-2) lors de la finale de Wimbledon en juillet 1998. C'était sa cinquième victoire sur ce court.

The Sampras
trademark slam
dunk, this time at
the Stella Artois
tournament, the
Queen's Club,
London,
11 June 1999.

Der für Sampras
typische Volley-
Schlag, diesmal beim
Stella-Artois-Turnier
des Londoner
Queen's Club,
11. Juni 1999.

Le smash de
Sampras, cette fois
au tournoi Stella
Artois organisé
au Queen's Club
de Londres,
le 11 juin 1999.

CLIVE BRUNSKILL/ALLSPORT

Runners in the
Berlin Marathon
of 1990, the first
to take place since
the Berlin Wall
was dismantled.

Das Teilnehmerfeld
beim Berlin-Mara-
thon von 1990, dem
ersten nach dem Fall
der Mauer.

Les concurrents du
Marathon de Berlin
de 1990, première
compétition organi-
sée dans la capitale
allemande depuis la
chute du Mur.

RICK STEWART/ALLSPORT

James Hastie takes out Andre Reed as the Buffalo Bills lose their Superbowl game against the New York Jets at Rich Stadium, the Bills' home ground, 1990.

Andre Reed hat das Nachsehen gegen James Hastie bei der Superbowl-Niederlage der Buffalo Bills gegen die New York Jets im Rich Stadium, Heimat der Buffalo Bills, 1990.

Un tampon de James Hastie sur Andre Reed lors du Superbowl de 1990, organisé au Rich Stadium, et que perdirent les Buffalo Bills sur leur terrain face aux New York Jets.

Sammy Sosa hits
his 63rd home run
of the season as
the Chicago Cubs
beat the San Diego
Padres 4-3,
Qualcomm Stadium,
San Diego,
17 September 1998.

Sammy Sosa holt
beim 4:3-Sieg der
Chicago Cubs gegen
die San Diego Padres
zu seinem 63. Home-
run der Saison aus,
Qualcomm Stadion,
San Diego,
17. September 1998.

Sammy Sosa marque
son 63ᵉ home run de
la saison lors de la
victoire par 4 à 3 des
Chicago Cubs sur les
San Diego Padres au
Qualcomm Stadium
de San Diego, le
17 septembre 1998.

Participants on the
eighth stage of the
1994 *Tour de France*
speed between fields
of sunflowers
near Poitiers.

Die Teilnehmer
der achten Etappe
bei der 1994er
Tour de France
sprinten durch die
Sonnenblumenfelder
nahe Poitiers.

Les coureurs de la
huitième étape du
Tour de France 1994
traversent des
champs de tourne-
sols près de Poitiers.

A jubilant Michael Johnson celebrates his 200 metres world record in the Olympic Games, Atlanta, Georgia, 1 August 1996.

Ein jubelnder Michael Johnson feiert seinen Weltrekord über 200 Meter bei den Olympischen Spielen von Atlanta, Georgia, 1. August 1996.

Michael Johnson jubile après avoir battu le record du monde du 200 mètres lors des Jeux olympiques d'Atlanta (Georgie), le 1ᵉʳ août 1996.

MIKE POWELL/ALLSPORT

Carl Lewis completes the United States' victory in the men's 4x100 metres relay at the Barcelona Olympics, August 1992. The US team set a new world record with a time of 37.40 seconds.

Carl Lewis macht den Triumph der 4 x 100-Meter-Staffel bei den Olympischen Spielen von Barcelona perfekt, August 1992. Das US-Team holte mit 37,40 Sekunden einen neuen Weltrekord.

Carl Lewis remporte la victoire pour les États-Unis dans le relais 4 x 100 mètres aux Olympiades de Barcelone, en août 1992. L'équipe américaine battit le record du monde avec un temps de 37,40 secondes.

Competitors in the
Ironman Triathlon
whip themselves
into a lather as they
take to the water,
Hawaii, 1991.

Die Schaum schla-
gende Konkurrenz
des Ironman-
Triathlon stürzt
sich ins Wasser,
Hawaii, 1991.

Les concurrents du
Triathlon Ironman
brassent l'écume
au départ de la
course, donné à
Hawaii en 1991.

11. Children
Kinder
Les enfants

At the height of the Kosovo crisis, a young ethnic Albanian refugee holds a Russian-made shell-case in his arms near the village of Kisna Reka, 12 October 1998.

Auf dem Höhepunkt der Kosovo-Krise hält ein junger albanischer Flüchtling nahe der Stadt Kisna Reka eine russische Granatenhülse in seinen Armen, 12. Oktober 1998.

Au plus fort de la crise du Kosovo, un jeune réfugié d'origine albanaise tient dans ses bras un obus de fabrication russe tombé près du village de Kisna Reka, le 12 octobre 1998.

11. Children
   Kinder
   Les enfants

Childhood became a frenetic race to grow up. There was less time to play with toys before children were expected to play their part in fostering a nation's economy – as consumers of designer clothes, discs, snacks, drinks, PlayStations. Child prodigies sat more examinations at earlier ages than ever before, exceptionally were accepted by universities before reaching their teens, delivered bravura performances at musical recitals. The old evils of the past reappeared. Young children were overworked and underpaid in Third World sweatshops. Epidemics of killer diseases returned to slaughter the innocents. Child abuse was uncovered in the very institutions that had been set up to help children. And there was a new phenomenon – the establishment of armies of child warriors. Governments and rebels alike kidnapped boys and girls as young as 10 years old, trained them to kill, and sent them out to do battle for the 'cause'.

On a gentler note, children ate junk food, played Pokémon, pestered their parents for skateboards, worshipped the great, resisted their teachers, moaned, laughed, fought and dreamed that one day they would all be healthy, wealthy and wise.

Die Kindheit wurde zu einem rasenden Wettkampf um das Erwachsenwerden. Heranwachsenden ließ man nur wenig Zeit, sich mit Spielzeug zu beschäftigen. Man erwartete, dass sie früh ihren Beitrag zum Wohle der heimischen Wirtschaft leisteten – als Konsumenten von Designerkleidung, Platten, Snacks, Getränken, Playstations. „Wunderkinder" bestanden im zartesten Alter mehr Prüfungen als die Hochbegabten früherer Epochen. Sie wurden per Sonderregelung zur Universität zugelassen, noch bevor sie ihr zwölftes Lebensjahr vollendet hatten oder sie entwickelten sich zu erfolgreichen Konzertsängern. Die alten Übel der Vergangenheit tauchten wieder auf. Kinder schufteten für einen Hungerlohn in den

Ausbeuterbetrieben der Dritten Welt. Todbringende Krankheiten brachen aus, denen unschuldige Kinder zum Opfer fielen. Kindesmissbrauch wurde ausgerechnet in jenen Institutionen aufgedeckt, die gegründet wurden, um Kindern zu helfen. Zudem gab es neue Phänomene – Kinder-Armeen wurden aufgebaut. Regierung und Rebellen entführten zehnjährige Jungen und Mädchen, brachten ihnen bei zu töten und schickten sie in den Kampf um „die gerechte Sache".

Milde ausgedrückt: Kinder aßen ungesundes Fast Food, spielten Pokémon, bettelten ihre Eltern um Skateboards an, schwärmten für die 'Großen', ließen sich von den Lehrern nicht beeindrucken, beschwerten sich, lachten, kämpften und träumten, dass sie eines Tages alle gesund, reich und weise sein würden.

L'enfance devenait une frénétique course à l'âge adulte. À cette époque, les enfants s'amusaient moins longtemps avec leurs jouets et incarnaient de plus en plus tôt un rôle de prescripteur actif dans l'économie de la nation – en tant que consommateurs de vêtements, de disques, de sandwichs, de boissons, de PlayStations. Si certains enfants prodiges se présentaient à des examens plus jeunes qu'autrefois et obtenaient même parfois une dérogation pour entrer à l'université avant l'adolescence, d'autres offraient de fantastiques récitals de musique. Les démons du passé réapparaissaient. Dans le tiers-monde, de jeunes enfants surchargés de travail étaient exploités dans des ateliers clandestins. Des épidémies de maladies mortelles décimaient des innocents. On découvrait que des adolescents avaient été abusés à l'intérieur de ces mêmes institutions qui étaient destinées à les protéger et les aider. Et on assistait à la naissance d'un nouveau phénomène : la création d'armées d'adolescents. Des gouvernements et des rebelles de tous bords kidnappaient des garçons et des filles de dix ans pour les entraîner à tuer et les renvoyer se battre pour la « cause ».

À un autre niveau, moins dramatique peut-être, les enfants s'habituaient à manger des cochonneries, jouaient au Pokémon, harcelaient leurs parents pour avoir un skate-board, vénéraient les vedettes, résistaient à leurs professeurs, geignaient, riaient, se battaient et rêvaient qu'un jour ils seraient tous en bonne santé, riches et sages.

EPA/PA

Enough to go round. Seven-year-old Besart Javori (centre) shares the delights of a juicy watermelon with his friends in a tractor trailer on a farm near the spa town of Banje, central Kosovo, 22 July 1999.

Genug für alle. Der siebenjährige Besart Javori (Mitte) teilt den Genuss einer fruchtigen Wassermelone mit seinen Freunden. Die Kinder sitzen in einem Traktoren-Anhänger auf einer Farm nahe dem Kurort Banje, im mittleren Kosovo, 22. Juli 1999.

Suffisamment pour chacun. Installés dans une remorque, Besart Javori (au centre), âgé de sept ans, et ses amis se délectent d'une pastèque dans une ferme proche de la ville balnéaire de Banje, au centre du Kosovo, le 22 juillet 1999.

Not enough
to go round.
A malnourished
child nibbles rations
supplied by the
World Food
Programme,
Luanda, Angola,
10 February 1999.

Nicht genug, um
über die Runden zu
kommen. Ein unter-
ernährtes Kind
knabbert an einer
Essensration, die
im Rahmen des
Welt-Lebensmittel-
programms bereit-
gestellt wurde,
Luanda, Angola,
10. Februar 1999.

Pas assez pour tous.
Cet enfant dénutri
grignote des rations
fournies par le
Programme alimen-
taire mondial, à
Luanda (Angola),
le 10 février 1999.

MANUEL DE ALMEIDA/EPA/PA

CHIEN-MIN CHUNG/LIAISON AGENCY

Formative years 1. Chinese children rub the
doorknobs on the gate leading to the Temple of
Heaven, Beijing, 5 August 1997, an action supposed
to bring good luck.

Prägende Jahre 1. Chinesische Kinder reiben an dem
Türknopf des Tores des Himmelstempels – eine Geste,
die Glück bringen soll, Peking, 5. August 1997.

Les années de formation I. Ces petits Chinois caressent
les boutons de la porte du Temple du Ciel à Pékin,
le 5 août 1997, un acte sensé porter chance.

Formative years 2. A photograph for the UN World Food Programme showing children with stunted growth in a North Korean nursery at Kumchon, Hwanghae province, 25 March 1999. Famine had hit this isolated region.

Prägende Jahre 2. Eine Fotografie im Auftrag des Welt-Lebensmittelprogramms der Vereinten Nationen zeigt Kinder einer Tagesstätte in der nordkoreanischen Stadt Kumchon, Provinz Hwanghae, deren Wachstum gehemmt ist, 25. März 1999. Eine Hungersnot hatte diese abgeschiedene Region heimgesucht.

Les années de formation II. Cette photographie du Programme alimentaire mondial des Nations Unies montre des enfants d'une crèche de Kumchon, dans la province de Hwanghae (Corée du Nord), atteints de rachitisme, après que la famine a touché cette région isolée, le 25 mars 1999.

Sudden death. Serb teenagers at the funerals of six friends killed in battles between Serbs and the Kosovo Liberation Army, 16 December 1998.

Plötzlicher Tod. Serbische Jugendliche bei der Beerdigung von sechs Freunden, die im Kampf zwischen den Serben und der Kosovo-Befreiungsarmee getötet wurden, 16. Dezember 1998.

Mort soudaine. Des adolescents serbes lors de l'enterrement de six de leurs camarades, tués dans une bataille entre les Serbes et l'Armée de Libération du Kosovo, le 16 décembre 1998.

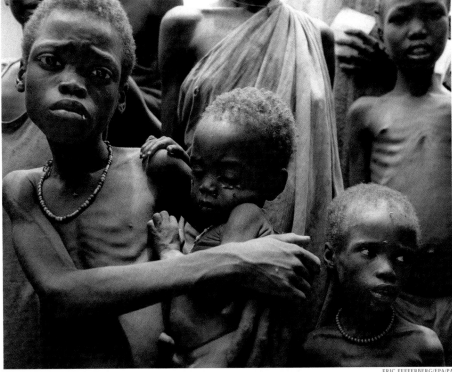

ERIC FEFFERBERG/EPA/PA

A lifetime of war. Sudanese children wait at a healthcare centre in Wau, southern Sudan, 20 July 1998. By then the war between the Sudanese Government and the Sudan People's Liberation Army had been going on for fifteen years.

Lebenslang Krieg. Sudanesische Kinder warten vor einem Gesundheitszentrum in Wau, im südlichen Sudan, 20. Juli 1998. Zu diesem Zeitpunkt wütete der Krieg zwischen der sudanesischen Regierung und der sudanesischen Befreiungsarmee seit bereits 15 Jahren.

Toute une vie en guerre. Des enfants soudanais attendent dans un centre de soins de Wau, au sud du Soudan, le 20 juillet 1998. Cela faisait 15 ans que durait la guerre entre le gouvernement soudanais et l'Armée de Libération du Peuple soudanais.

SIMON NORFOLK/PYMCA

The facts of life. A school pupil displays a condom to his classmates as part of a sex education and anti-AIDS programme. If you doubt the propriety of such happenings, study the page opposite.

Fakten des Lebens. Ein Schüler zeigt seinen Klassenkameraden ein Kondom. Die Aufklärung über Verhütungsmethoden ist Teil des Sexualkundeunterrichts und des Anti-Aids-Programms. Sie finden diese Art der Vorbeugung übertrieben? Schauen Sie sich die gegenüberliegende Seite an!

Dans la vie réelle. Un écolier montre un préservatif à sa classe dans le cadre du programme d'éducation sexuelle et antisida. Si vous doutez de l'intérêt de tels cours, regardez la page suivante.

EPA/PA

Kenyan children at the Kikoshep school in the slum area of Kibera, Nairobi, 29 November 1998. All have lost at least one parent to AIDS; all are carrying the HIV virus.

Kenianische Kinder der Kikoshep-Schule im Elendsviertel von Kibera, Nairobi, 29. November 1998. Alle Schüler haben mindestens ein Elternteil an Aids verloren. Jeder von ihnen trägt das HIV-Virus in sich.

Des élèves kenyans de l'école Kikoshep, installée dans un quartier pauvre de Kibera, à Nairobi, le 29 novembre 1998. Tous ont perdu au moins un parent à cause du sida, et tous sont porteurs du virus HIV.

An AWB gathering
on the 'Day of the
Vow', Pretoria,
South Africa,
5 December 1993.
Afrikaaners celebrate
a victory over the
Zulus in 1838.

Eine Versammlung
der rechtsradikalen
Afrikaaner Weer-
standsbeweging
(AWB) am „Tag
des Gelübdes" in
Pretoria, Südafrika,
5. Dezember 1993.
Afrikaans spre-
chende, in Südafrika
geborene Weiße
feiern den Sieg
über die Zulu im
Jahr 1838.

Un rassemblement
de l'AWB à Pretoria
(Afrique du Sud),
le « Jour du Vœu »,
le 5 décembre 1993.
Les Afrikanders célé-
braient une victoire
sur les Zoulous
datant de 1838.

DAVID BRAUCHLI/LIAISON AGENCY

DAVID BRAUCHLI/LIAISON AGENCY

A young boy in a Sarajevo food store, 14 June 1995. At the time Sarajevans were stocking up on basic supplies in the belief that Bosnian and Serb troops would soon be fighting north of their city.

Ein kleiner Junge in einem Lebensmittelgeschäft in Sarajevo, 14. Juni 1995. Zu dieser Zeit hortete die Bevölkerung Sarajevos Grundnahrungsmittel, weil man befürchtete, dass sich bosnische und serbische Truppen bald nördlich der Stadt Gefechte liefern würden.

Un jeune garçon dans un magasin d'alimentation de Sarajevo, le 14 juin 1995. Les habitants de Sarajevo stockaient alors les produits de première nécessité en pensant que les troupes bosniaques et serbes allaient bientôt s'affronter au nord de leur ville.

ROBERT SEMENIUK/BLACK STAR/COLORIFIC!

Children have always played with toy guns: these are home-made replicas of
M-16s. Palestinian children traumatised by years of fighting and killing re-enact
Intifada with a game called 'Arabs and Jews'.

Kinder haben schon immer mit Spielzeuggewehren gespielt: Unser Bild zeigt
selbst gebaute M-16-Nachbildungen. Palästinensische Kinder, traumatisiert
von den Jahren des Kämpfens und Tötens, üben die Intifada (den Aufstand).
„Araber und Juden" heißt ihr Spiel.

Les enfants ont toujours aimé jouer avec des armes, même factices, comme ces
répliques artisanales de M-16. Ces jeunes Palestiniens, traumatisés par des années
de luttes et de tueries, rejouent à l'Intifada dans un jeu appelé « Arabes et Juifs ».

A Sunday morning militia training exercise in Cuba, 1990. The most powerful nations in the world rightly disapproved of the practice of arming children, but none of them was prepared to do anything to stop it.

Eine militärische Übung an einem Sonntagmorgen des Jahres 1990 in Kuba. Die mächtigsten Nationen der Welt haben die militärische Ausbildung von Kindern zwar zu Recht verurteilt, doch kein einziger Staat hat sich bislang bemüht, etwas dagegen zu tun.

Exercice dominical de la milice, à Cuba en 1990. Si les nations les plus puissantes du monde désapprouvaient à juste titre la pratique d'armer les enfants, aucune d'entre elles n'était prête à faire quoi que ce soit pour l'empêcher vraiment.

Junior Zoegee
sets off to war.
The 13-year-old
was on his way
through Monrovia,
to fight Liberian
Government troops,
July 1990.

Der kleine Zoegee
zieht in den Krieg.
Unser Bild zeigt den
13-Jährigen im Juli
des Jahres 1990,
als er quer durch
Monrovia fährt,
um gegen die
Regierungstruppen
Liberias zu kämpfen.

Junior Zoegee
part en guerre. Ce
gamin de 13 ans se
rendait à Monrovia
pour combattre
les troupes du gou-
vernement libérien,
en juillet 1990.

BEAWIHARTA/REUTERS/ARCHIVE PHOTOS

Australian troops of the International Forces for East Timor file past children near Dili, 21 September 1999. It was hoped that the new generation would be spared the horrors of a war that had already lasted twenty-four years.

Kinder in Dili am 21. September 1999. Im Hintergrund: marschierende australische Soldaten der Internationalen Streitkräfte für Osttimor. Man hatte gehofft, dass der jungen Generation die Schrecken eines Krieges erspart bleiben würden, der schon 24 Jahre andauert.

Des enfants et des soldats australiens de la Force internationale pour le Timor Oriental, près de Dili, le 21 septembre 1999. On espérait épargner à la nouvelle génération les horreurs d'une guerre qui durait déjà depuis 24 ans.

Young girls prepare to dance at a Buddhist festival in Hong Kong to celebrate reunification with China, 1 July 1997.

Eine Gruppe kleiner Mädchen bereitet sich auf ihren Auftritt vor. Bei einem buddhistischen Festival in Hongkong, zur Feier der Wiedervereinigung mit China, werden sie einen Tanz aufführen, 1. Juli 1997.

Ces petites filles se préparent à danser lors d'une fête bouddhiste à Hong-Kong célébrant la réunification avec la Chine, le 1er juillet 1997.

MANFRED HORVATH/ANZENBERGER/COLORIFIC!

The best playgrounds are always those that are discovered, adopted, adapted, taken over. Young bicycle acrobats take delightedly to the waters of the Stadwäldchen, Budapest, Hungary.

Die besten Spielplätze sind diejenigen, die man selbst findet, erfindet und seinen Bedürfnissen anpasst. Unser Bild zeigt junge Fahrradakrobaten, die sich begeistert in das Gewässer des Stadwäldchens in Budapest, Ungarn, stürzen.

Les meilleurs terrains de jeux sont toujours ceux qui sont inventés, adoptés, adaptés et envahis. Ces jeunes cyclistes acrobates plongent avec délices dans les eaux du Stadwäldchen de Budapest, en Hongrie.

RUSSEL TADICH/LIAISON AGENCY

Undismayed by the bullet-scarred walls around them, Serb children play football in the ruins of Vukovar, November 1996. The town was destroyed during fighting between Yugoslav and Croatian forces.

Ohne sich um die von Einschusslöchern übersäten Wände um sie herum zu kümmern, spielen serbische Kinder in den Ruinen von Vukovar im November 1996 Fußball. Die Stadt wurde während der Kämpfe zwischen der jugoslawischen und der kroatischen Armee zerstört.

Peu impressionnés par les traces de balles sur les murs, des enfants serbes jouent au football dans les ruines de Vukovar, en novembre 1996. La ville fut détruite lors des combats entre forces yougoslaves et croates.

(Opposite) Aweys Mohamed, 12, landmine victim, Somalia, 1999. (Right) A 12-year-old handicapped Bedouin – 'the family's shame', 1990.

Der zwölfjährige Aweys Mohamed (gegenüberliegende Seite) wurde Opfer einer Landmine, Somalia, 1999. (Rechts) Ein 12-jähriger, behinderter Beduine – „die Schande der Familie", 1990.

(Ci-contre) Aweys Mohamed, 12 ans, victime d'une mine en Somalie, en 1999. (À droite) Un Bédouin handicapé de 12 ans – la « honte de la famille » – en 1990.

NITSAN SHORER/BLACK STAR/COLORIFIC!

A young Muslim boy is prepared for a visit to the family patriarch, Afghanistan, 1992. He appears adjusted to the importance and solemnity of the occasion.

Ein kleiner muslimischer Junge wird auf den Besuch des Familienoberhaupts vorbereitet, Afghanistan, 1992. Der feierlichen Bedeutung dieses Anlasses scheint sich der Kleine bewusst zu sein.

On habille ce jeune musulman avant sa visite au patriarche de la famille, en Afghanistan, en 1992. Il semble très conscient de l'importance et de la solennité du moment.

12. All human life
Menschliches, Allzumenschliches
Les petits et les grands événements de la vie

Seven-month-old Dolly, the world's first cloned animal, stands proudly in her
pen at Edinburgh's Roslin Institute, 23 February 1997.

Die sieben Monate alte Dolly, das erste geklonte Tier der Welt, steht stolz in
ihrem Verschlag im Roslin Institute in Edinburgh, 23. Februar 1997.

Dolly, une brebis de sept mois et le premier animal cloné au monde, se tient
fièrement dans son étable du Roslin Institute d'Édimbourg, le 23 février 1997.

12. All human life
Menschliches, Allzumenschliches
Les petits et les grands événements de la vie

As the century drew to a close, what was there left for human beings to invent, discover, demand, treasure or ill-use? It was a time of nostalgia. People recreated old journeys – walking across the Antarctic in the steps of Amundsen, Shackleton and Scott; sailing round the world in the wake of Drake and Magellan; climbing Everest in the ghoulish hope of finding the frozen remains of those who had perished in earlier attempts. It was time once again to plunder the carcass of the *Titanic*, search for the skeletons of planes shot down in the Second World War, restore old locomotives and revive the classic excursions by steam trains of the 1930s.

There were new vogues, new fads – the Trabant and the Jeep, smoked vegetables and ostrich meat, wild gardens and exotic pets, collecting telephone cards and Cold War memorabilia. And there were new problems. Mountains were being eroded by the very climbers they attracted. Venice was still sinking beneath the weight of its own tourists. Dozens of other glories had to be placed out of bounds to souvenir hunters.

And, at the Kyoto Conference in 1998, world leaders began the arduous process of rationing the world's energy resources…

Was konnten die Menschen noch erfinden, entdecken, verlangen, wertschätzen oder missbrauchen, als sich das Jahrhundert dem Ende zuneigte? Es war eine Zeit der Nostalgie. Einige ließen alte Reiserouten wieder auferstehen und wanderten in den Fußstapfen von Amundsen, Shackleton und Scott durch die Antarktis. Andere segelten um die Welt wie Drake und Magellan. Wieder andere bestiegen den Mount Everest mit dem makabren Wunsch, die gefrorenen Überreste jener Bergsteiger zu finden, die dort bei früheren Expeditionen umkamen. Erneut machten sich Tauchtrupps auf, das Wrack der *Titanic* zu plündern, erneut begann die Suche nach Flugzeugen, die im Zweiten Weltkrieg abgeschossen worden waren. Alte Lokomotiven wurden restauriert und Ausflüge mit dampfbetriebenen Eisenbahnen aus den dreißiger Jahren erneut ins Leben gerufen.

Es gab neue Modewellen und Marotten – der Trabant und der Jeep, geräuchertes Gemüse und Straußenfleisch, Naturgärten und exotische Haustiere, Telefonkartensammler und Reminiszenzen an den Kalten Krieg. Und es gab neue Probleme: zum Beispiel Bodenerosionen in den Gebirgen, ausgelöst von Kletterern, die es in die Berge zog. Venedig sank weiter unter dem Gewicht seiner Touristen. Dutzende anderer Sehenswürdigkeiten mussten vor Souvenirjägern geschützt werden.

Und auf der Kyoto-Konferenz des Jahres 1998 legten die Mächtigen der Welt den Grundstein für den mühsamen Prozess der Rationierung vorhandener Energieressourcen.

Le siècle touchant à sa fin, que restait-il à inventer, découvrir, revendiquer, conserver ou maltraiter ? L'époque était à la nostalgie. Certains recommençaient d'anciennes aventures : la traversée de l'Antarctique sur les traces d'Amundsen, de Shackleton ou de Scott, le tour du monde en bateau dans le sillage de Drake et de Magellan, ou l'ascension de l'Everest dans l'espoir macabre de découvrir les restes gelés de tous ceux qui y avaient péri lors de précédentes tentatives. D'autres replongeaient dans le passé : pour fouiller l'épave du *Titanic*, rechercher des carcasses d'avions de la Seconde Guerre mondiale, restaurer de vieilles locomotives et reprendre les classiques excursions en train à vapeur des années 1930.

Il y avait de nouvelles vogues, de nouvelles marottes : la Trabant et la Jeep, les légumes fumés et la viande d'autruche, les jardins sauvages et les animaux exotiques, les collections de cartes téléphoniques et les souvenirs de la guerre froide. Et de nouveaux problèmes émergeaient. Les montagnes étaient rabotées par les nombreux alpinistes qu'elles attiraient. Venise s'enfonçait encore un peu plus sous le poids de ses touristes. Des dizaines d'autres souvenirs glorieux devaient être placés hors d'atteinte des chasseurs de souvenirs.

Et, à la Conférence de Kyoto de 1998, les dirigeants du monde envisageaient de rationner les ressources énergétiques du monde …

DESMOND BOYLAN/REUTERS/ARCHIVE PHOTOS

Every bad comedian's nightmare. Inhabitants of Buñol, near Valencia,
Spain, flounder in the pulp of the 100 tonnes of tomatoes they have
hurled at each other during their local festival, 28 August 1996.

Albtraum jedes schlechten Komikers. Bewohner des spanischen Ortes
Buñol, nahe Valencia, waten durch 100 Tonnen Tomatenmasse.
Während ihres Ortsfestes am 28. August 1996 bewarfen sich die
Feiernden gegenseitig mit dem roten Gemüse.

Le cauchemar de tous les mauvais comédiens. Les habitants de Buñol,
près de Valence (Espagne), s'ébattent dans la pulpe des 100 tonnes de
tomates qu'ils se sont lancées lors de leur fête locale, le 28 août 1996.

JIM HOLLANDER/REUTERS/ARCHIVE PHOTOS

In drunken memory of Ernest Hemingway. A visitor to the Fiesta de San Fermín, when the bulls run through the streets of Pamplona, dives confidently into the arms of waiting friends, 6 July 1999.

Trunkene Erinnerung an Ernest Hemingway. Während der Fiesta de San Fermín, bei der Stiere durch die Straßen von Pamplona getrieben werden, lässt sich ein Besucher vertrauensvoll in die Arme wartender Freunde fallen, 6. Juli 1999.

En mémoire de Ernest Hemingway. Un participant à la Fiesta de San Fermín à Pampelune, au cours de laquelle les taureaux courent dans les rues de la ville, plonge avec confiance dans les bras de ses amis, le 6 juillet 1999.

JERRY LAMPEN/REUTERS/ARCHIVE PHOTOS

(Above) A hurricane visit. Polish bishops battered by the rotor wash from the Pope's helicopter as they await his arrival in Elblag, Poland, 6 June 1999. (Opposite) Casting their fates to the winds. Graduates of the Air Force Academy commencement maintain the old tradition as they hurl their caps into the air, 2 June 1999.

(Oben) Stürmischer Besuch. Gebeutelt vom kräftigen Windzug, der von den Rotoren seines Helikopters ausgeht, erwarten polnische Bischöfe die Ankunft des Papstes in Elblag, Polen, 6. Juni 1999. (Gegenüberliegende Seite) Sie vertrauen ihr Schicksal dem Wind an. Absolventen der Luftwaffenakademie folgen bei der Abschlussfeier einer alten Tradition und werfen ihre Kappen in die Luft, 2. Juni 1999.

(Ci-dessus) Une visite en trombe. Les évêques polonais sont pris dans le souffle du rotor de l'hélicoptère du pape lors de son arrivée à Elblag (Pologne), le 6 juin 1999. (Ci-contre) Jeter sa foi aux quatre vents. Des officiers de l'Air Force Academy lors de la remise des diplômes perpétuent l'ancienne tradition de jeter leur casquette en l'air, le 2 juin 1999.

LAURENCE AGRON/ARCHIVE PHOTOS

Body-building. Kim Chivesky (USA – 1st) (left), Natalia Murnikoviene (Lithuania – 2nd) (centre) and Lenda Murray (USA – 3rd) (right) show what they're made of at the Ms Olympia Bodybuilding Contest, Chicago, 20 September 1996.

Bodybuilding. Kim Chivesky (USA, Nr. 1, links), Natalia Murnikoviene (Litauen, Nr. 2, Mitte) und Lenda Murray (USA, Nr. 3, rechts) zeigen beim Miss Olympia Bodybuilding-Wettbewerb in Chicago ihre Muskeln, 20. September 1996.

Montrer son corps. Kim Chivesky (États-Unis – 1re) (à gauche), Natalia Murnikoviene (Lituanie – 2e) (au centre) et Lenda Murray (États-Unis – 3e) (à droite) montrent ce qu'elles ont fait d'elles lors du concours de body-building de Mlle Olympia à Chicago, le 20 septembre 1996.

SAEED KHAN/EPA/PA

Body-hiding. Three members of the audience at an address by Benazir Bhutto, the deposed premier of Pakistan, Rattudero, 28 January 1997. The public meeting attracted a large number of women.

Versteckte Körper. Drei Zuhörerinnen bei einer Ansprache von Benazir Bhutto, der abgesetzten Premierministerin von Pakistan, in Rattudero, 28. Januar 1997. Die öffentliche Veranstaltung zog sehr viele Frauen an.

Cacher son visage. Trois des nombreuses Pakistanaises présentes lors d'un discours public de Benazir Bhutto, la Premier ministre, à Rattudero, le 28 janvier 1997.

WILLIAM BRETZGER/LIAISON AGENCY

The sincerest form of flattery. Some 2,000 Rocky Balboa impersonators mount the steps of Philadelphia's Museum of Art as part of the Millennium celebrations, 31 December 1999. They were recreating a scene from the movie *Rocky*.

Ehre, wem Ehre gebührt. Rund 2000 Rocky-Balboa-Doppelgänger erstürmen im Rahmen der Jahrtausendfeiern die Stufen des Kunstmuseums in Philadelphia, 31. Dezember 1999. Sie stellen eine Szene des Films *Rocky* nach.

La forme de flatterie la plus sincère. Près de 2000 sosies de Rocky Balboa montent les marches du Museum of Art de Philadelphie lors des célébrations du Millénaire, le 31 décembre 1999. Ils reprenaient ainsi une scène du film *Rocky*.

TIMOTHY J JONES/LIAISON AGENCY

'Down at the end of Lonely Street…at heart-attack hotel' Paul Rudy, the 'Jelly Doughnut Elvis', shakes it all about in the annual Elvis Parade on the anniversary of Presley's death, Kansas City, 16 August 1996.

„Down at the end of Lonely Street … at heart-attack hotel". Elvis-Darsteller Paul Rudy, der „Jelly Doughnut Elvis", gibt bei der jährlichen Parade am Todestag von Elvis Presley alles, Kansas City, 16. August 1996.

« Down at the end of lonely Street … at heart-attack hotel ». Paul Rudy, surnommé « Jelly Doughnut Elvis », se démène lors de la Parade Elvis annuelle organisée à l'occasion de l'anniversaire de la mort d'Elvis Presley à Kansas City, le 16 août 1996.

GEORGES DE KEERLE/LIAISON AGENCY

Fighting for a place in the market economy. Four young women
arrested for prostitution parade before Moscow police, May 1997.
Low wages drove many Russian women onto the streets.

Der Kampf um einen Platz in der Marktwirtschaft. Vier junge Frauen
werden wegen Prostitution von der Moskauer Polizeibehörde verhaftet,
Mai 1997. Wegen der niedrigen Gehälter gingen viele russische Frauen
auf die Straße.

Se faire une place dans l'économie de marché. Ces quatre jeunes femmes
ont été arrêtées pour prostitution par la police moscovite, en mai 1997.
Les bas salaires avaient mis de nombreuses Moscovites sur le trottoir.

E BOUVET/SAGA/COLORIFIC!

'For better, for worse…' Russian women examine the files of available talent at a Moscow marriage bureau, October 1992, each of them searching for an American husband.

„Gute Zeiten, schlechte Zeiten …" Russische Frauen durchforsten die Kartei eines Moskauer Ehevermittlungsinstituts nach möglichen Kandidaten, Oktober 1992. Sie alle suchen einen amerikanischen Ehemann.

« Pour le meilleur et pour le pire … » Des Russes examinent le fichier d'une agence matrimoniale de Moscou, en octobre 1992, à la recherche d'un mari américain.

More than 1,300
participants at a
mass wedding
ceremony in the
Pennsylvania
Convention Center,
31 December 1999.
Presumably all
ended up with their
intended partner.

Mehr als 1300
Teilnehmer einer
Massenhochzeits-
Zeremonie im
Convention Center
Pennsylvania,
31. Dezember 1999.
Mit ein wenig Glück
haben am Ende alle
den Partner ihrer
Wahl auch tatsäch-
lich geheiratet.

On a compté plus
de 1300 participants
à cette cérémonie de
mariages collectifs
organisée au
Pennsylvania Con-
vention Center, le
31 décembre 1999.
On suppose que
tout le monde a fini
la soirée avec le
partenaire prévu.

The turtle has landed. John H. Glenn Jnr simulates a parachute drop during training at the Sonny Carter Training Center.

Die Schildkröte fällt. John H. Glenn jun. simuliert einen Fallschirmsprung während einer Übung im Sonny Carter Training Center.

La tortue a atterri. John H. Glenn Jr. s'entraîne au largage en parachute au Sonny Carter Training Center.

NASA/ARCHIVE PHOTOS

Overturned turtles. Employees of a South Korean industrial instrument company participate in a morale-boosting workout on Daebu Island, 17 April 1998.

Schildkröten auf dem Rücken: Angestellte einer südkoreanischen Industriemaschinen-Firma nehmen an einem Training zur Motivationsförderung auf der Insel Daebu teil, 17. April 1998.

Des tortues retournées. Des employés d'une entreprise d'instruments industriels sud-coréenne participent à une séance de remise en forme sur l'île Daebu, le 17 avril 1998.

CHRIS BOURONCLE/EPA/PA

Native Chilean Indians take part in a march from Santiago to the National Congress in Valparaiso, 12 August 1998. They walked the 71 miles to protest against the building of a dam for hydroelectricity.

Indianische Ureinwohner Chiles nehmen an einem Protestzug teil, der von Santiago zum Nationalen Kongress in Valparaiso führt, 12. August 1998. Sie liefen die 71 Meilen, um gegen den Bau eines Staudamms für ein Wasserkraftwerk zu demonstrieren.

Des indiens du Chili participent à une marche entre Santiago et Valparaiso, où se tenait le Congrès national, le 12 août 1998. Ils parcoururent les 114 kilomètres à pied pour protester contre la construction d'un barrage hydroélectrique.

LEHTIKUVA OY/PA

Taking work home for the weekend. A Latvian executive strides along a stretch of beach at the Latvian Nudist Colony, Saule, 10 June 1992. After seventy years of Communism the whole exercise must have come as an enormous relief.

Arbeit mit ins Wochenende nehmen. Ein lettischer Abteilungsleiter streift über einen Strand der lettischen Nudistenkolonie von Saule, 10. Juni 1992. Nach 70 Jahren Kommunismus wohl eine der leichteren Übungen.

Du travail pour le week-end. Ce chef d'entreprise letton marche sur la plage qui borde la colonie nudiste de Saule (Lettonie), le 10 juin 1992. Après 70 ans de communisme, la pratique de ce simple exercice devait paraître une délivrance.

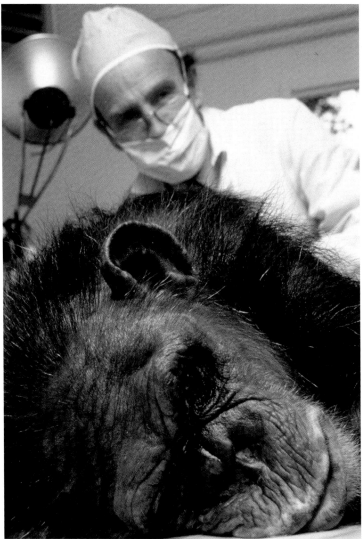

Doctor Jim Mahoney reluctantly submits an adult chimpanzee to AIDS research at the New York University Medical Center.

Zögernd führt Doctor Jim Mahoney an der New Yorker Universitätsklinik Untersuchungen an einem erwachsenen Schimpansen durch. Sie sollen der Erforschung von Aids dienen.

À contrecœur, le Dr Jim Mahoney procède à des recherches sur le sida sur un chimpanzé adulte au University Medical Center de New York.

The funeral of Sister Dinarosa Bellerini, an Italian nursing nun, Kikwit Hospital, Zaire, 15 May 1995. She was one of the first victims of an Ebola virus epidemic which struck central Africa for the first time in seventeen years.

Die Beerdigung von Schwester Dinarosa Bellerini, einer italienischen Krankenschwester und Nonne, Kikwit-Krankenhaus, Zaire, 15. Mai 1995. Sie war eines der ersten Opfer der Ebola-Virus-Epidemie, die sich in Zentralafrika – zum ersten Mal seit 17 Jahren – wieder ausbreitete.

Les funérailles de sœur Dinarosa Bellerini, une infirmière italienne du Kikwit Hospital (Zaïre), le 15 mai 1995. Elle fut l'une des premières victimes de l'épidémie du virus Ebola qui frappa l'Afrique centrale pour la première fois en 17 ans.

384 All human life

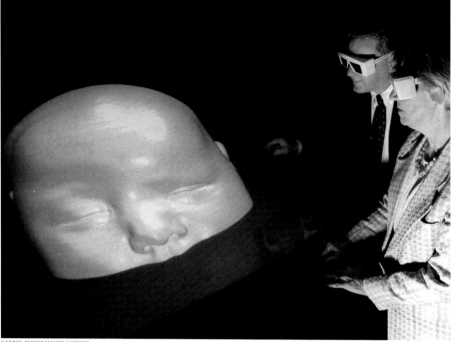

DARRYL BUSH/LIAISON AGENCY

Bulging baby image. Doctor Muriel Ross of NASA (right) and Dr Stephen
S Schendel examine a 3D scan of a baby's head at NASA's Ames Research
Center, 26 March 1997.

Ein wuchtiges Bild von einem Baby. Doktor Muriel Ross von der NASA (rechts)
und Doktor Stephen S. Schendel betrachten den 3-D-Scan eines Baby-Kopfes im
Ames Research Center der NASA, 26. März 1997.

Naissance d'un bébé virtuel. Le Dr Muriel Ross, de la NASA (à droite) et le
Dr Stephen S. Schendel examinent une scanographie en 3D de la tête d'un bébé
au Ames Research Center de la NASA, le 26 mars 1997.

By the 1990s the computer was beginning to expand its impact on the world. Virtual reality was the name given by the ignorant to 'Cyberworld'. (Above) Visitors from Cyberworld take a trip back home.

In den 1990er Jahren wuchs die Bedeutung des Computers weltweit. Nur Unwissende hielten die Cyberworld für „virtuelle Realität". (Oben) Besucher der Cyberworld auf dem „Trip" nach Hause.

L'ordinateur commença à étendre son influence sur le monde dans les années 1990. Les ignorants désignaient par « réalité virtuelle » ce que les savants appelaient « Cyberworld ». (Ci-dessus) Des visiteurs du Cyberworld en plein fantasme virtuel.

DotComGuy, the
Texan who decided
to live his whole life
through the net,
16 December 1999.
At least e-mail
Christmas cards
don't fall off the
mantelpiece.

DotComGuy,
der Texaner, der
sich entschloss,
sein ganzes Leben
über das Internet
zu gestalten,
16. Dezember 1999.
Zumindest können
E-Mail-Weihnachts-
karten nicht vom
Kaminsims fallen.

DotComGuy est
un Texan qui décida
de vivre toute sa
vie sur le net, le
16 décembre 1999.
Au moins, les cartes
de Noël qu'il reçoit
par e-mail ne
tombent plus de
la cheminée.

PAUL MILLER/BLACK STAR/COLORIFIC!

Three hundred thousand bikers invade the town of Sturgis, N. Dakota
(pop. 7,000), for the 50th anniversary of the Black Hills Motor Classic.
Every summer for a week Sturgis opens its minds, hearts and doors to bikers.

300 000 Biker fallen zum 50. Black Hills Motor Classic in die Stadt Sturgis in
Nord-Dakota ein, die selbst nur 7000 Einwohner zählt. Jeden Sommer bietet die
Stadt eine Woche lang all ihre Gastfreundschaft auf, die Biker zu beherbergen.

Trois cent mille « bikers » envahissent la ville de Sturgis (7000 hab.), dans le
Dakota du Nord, pour le 50ᵉ anniversaire du Black Hills Motor Classic.
Chaque été pendant une semaine, Sturgis ouvre son esprit, son cœur et sa porte
aux motards.

JOSEPH RODRIGUEZ/BLACK STAR/COLORIFIC!

A tenement block in the photographer's own El Barrio district of East Harlem, New York City. The windows have been decorated with soft toys by parents as a sign of defiance against local crack dealers.

Ein Mietwohnblock im Distrikt El Barrio in East Harlem, New York City, in dem der Fotograf selbst wohnt. Eltern haben die Fenster mit Stofftieren dekoriert – als Zeichen des Widerstands gegen die Crack-Dealer aus der Gegend.

Un immeuble d'appartements du Barrio, le quartier de East Harlem à New York où habite le photographe. Les jouets en peluche aux fenêtres manifestent l'opposition des parents aux vendeurs de crack locaux.

The usual queue
in the Ladies.
Flamingos shelter
from Hurricane
George in the
restroom of Miami's
Metro Zoo,
25 September 1998.

Die übliche Schlange
auf dem Damenklo.
Diese Flamingos
suchen auf der
Toilette des Metro-
Zoos in Miami
Schutz vor dem
Hurrikan George,
25. September 1998.

Affluence habituelle
dans les toilettes des
dames. Des flamands
roses se sont abrités
de l'ouragan George
dans les toilettes du
zoo de Miami, le
25 septembre 1998.

Index

gettyimages

Over 70 million images and 30,000 hours of film footage are held by the various collections owned by Getty Images. These cover a vast number of subjects from the earliest photojournalism to current press photography, sports, social history and geography. Getty Images' conceptual imagery is renowned amongst creative end users.
www.gettyimages.com

Über 70 Millionen Bilder und 30 000 Stunden Film befinden sich in den verschiedenen Archiven von Getty Images. Sie decken ein breites Spektrum an Themen ab – von den ersten Tagen des Fotojournalismus bis hin zu aktueller Pressefotografie, Sport, Sozialgeschichte und Geographie. Bei kreativen Anwendern ist das Material von Getty Images für seine ausdrucksstarke Bildsprache bekannt.
www.gettyimages.com

Plus de 70 millions d'images et 30 000 heures de films sont détenus par les différentes collections dont Getty Images est le propriétaire. Cela couvre un nombre considérable de sujets – des débuts du photojournalisme aux photographies actuelles de presse, de sport, d'histoire sociale et de géographie. Le concept photographique de Getty Images est reconnu des créatifs.
www.gettyimages.com

Acknowledgements

The picture editor is grateful to the following individuals and agencies or collections with which they are associated for their assistance with this book:

Christopher Angeloglou, Julius Domoney, David Leverton and Sally Ryall (Colorific!); Anh Stack and Michelle Hernandez (Black Star); Rosa Di Salvo, Richard Ellis, Bob Hechler, Hilary Johnston, Robert Pepper, Eric Smalkin (Liaison Agency); Rob Harborne, Lee Martin and Matthew Stevens (Allsport); Mitch Blank, Kathy Lavelle, Eric Rachlis, Peter Rohowsky and Arlete Santos (Hulton|Archive, New York); Antonia Hille, Sarah Kemp and Alex Linghorn (Hulton|Archive, London); Jake Cunningham (PYMCA); Martin Stephens and Milica Timotic (PA News); Gul Duzyol and Jocelyne Manfredi (Sipa Press); Judith Caul and Tony Mancini (*The Guardian*); Jim Docherty and Marianne Lassen (S.I.N.); Simon Kenton (Idols); and to Sara Green and Stephanie Hudson for their kind assistance in New York and London respectively.